Observations on Several Parts of England, Particularly the Mountains and Lakes of Cumberland and Westmoreland, Relative Chiefly to Picturesque Beauty, Made in the Year 1772

OBSERVATIONS,

ON

SEVERAL PARTS OF ENGLAND,

PARTICULARLY THE

MOUNTAINS AND LAKES

OF

Cumberland and Westmoreland,

RELATIVE CHIEFLY TO

PICTURESQUE BEAUTY,

MADE IN THE YEAR 1772.

By WILLIAM GILPIN, A.M.
PREBENDARY OF SALISBURY; AND VICAR OF BOLDRE IN
NEW-FOREST, NEAR LYMINGTON.

THE THIRD EDITION, IN TWO VOLUMES.
VOL. II.

LONDON:
PRINTED FOR T. CADELL AND W. DAVIES, STRAND.
1808.

Strahan and Preston,
Printers-Street, London.

CONTENTS

OF

THE SECOND VOLUME.

SECTION XVI.

BUTERMER lower lake. 1 — mountain of Grafmer. 3 — account of an inundation. 4 — defcription of the vale of Lorton. 7 — difficulty of verbal defcription. 9 — difficulty alfo of picturefque defcription. 10 — in what the perfection of painting confifts. 11 — why a fketch pleafes. 14 — a fuppofition of Mr. Burke's criticized. 15 — different kinds of landfcape require different modes of light. 17 — defcription of a tempeftuous night in a mountainous country. 20 — images of the fame kind from Croma. 22.

SECT. XVII.

Druid temple. 27 — remarks on proper and improper, fubjects for painting. 29 — defcription of the vale of St. John. 31 — compared with the vale of Tempe. 33 — violent inundation. 36 — paffage over mountains. 38 — extenfive vale. 40 — ideas of fpace, not always adapted to little scenes. 40 — a road, and a river compared, as objects of beauty. 41 — Wolf's-cragg. 42 — remarks on figures in landscape. 43.

SECT. XVIII.

Description of a gill, or ravine. 49 — first view of Ullefwater. 50 — description of it. 50 — full view of it 52 — Mr. Burke's idea of the sublime criticized. 53 — reflections on sounds, (grand, or musical,) as adapted to scenery. 58 — Stibra-cragg. 63 — village of Patterdale. 64 — the simplicity of the country exemplified in an anecdote of a clergyman. 65 — the great mischief of introducing dissipation into it. 67.

SECT. XIX.

Description of Ullefwater under the circumstance of a perfect calm. 72 — description of a rocky pass, called Yew-cragg. 75 — two circular vallies. 77 — hill of Dunmallet. 80 — village of Water-mullock. 81 — view towards Pooly-bridge. 82 — effect of moonlight. 82 — an uncommon fish in Ullefwater. 83 — Dacre-castle. 84 — Penrith-castle, and beacon. 85 — town of Penrith. 86 — Inglewood forest. 87 — story of bishop Nicolson. 88 — Roman works at Plumpton, and Ragmire. 89 — approach to Carlisle. 90.

SECT. XX.

City of Carlisle. 93 — anecdote relative to the siege it sustained in 1745. 97 — vale of Dalston. 100 — Rosecastle.

castle. 101 — inscription at Chalk-cliff. 101 — Corby-castle. 102 — Warwick. 107.

SECT. XXI.

Description of Brugh-marsh. 109 — death of Edward I. 112 — view from Stanwix-bank. 114 — Naworth-castle. 115 — Lord William Howard. 116 — abbey of Lanercost. 118 — rivers characterized. 120 — description of Scaleby-castle. 121.

SECT. XXII.

Netherby. 127 — ancient state of the borders. 128 — present state 129 — account of the over-flowing of Solway-moss. 133 — methods taken to clear it. 143.

SECT. XXIII.

Vale of Lowther. 145 — Brougham-castle. 145 — Clifton. 146 — Lowther-hall. 147 — Appelby-castle. 147 — observations on smaller objects, detached from larger. 148 — account of the celebrated Lady Dowager Pembroke. 149.

SECT. XXIV.

Observations on a formal piece of ground near Brugh. 165 — Brugh-castle. 166 — remarks on the colouring of nature. 167 — Bowes-castle. 168 — Gatherly moor, and the various picturesque distances it affords. 171 — story of king James I. 172 — Leeming-lane. 173.

SECT. XXV.

Studley. 175 — the idea, which the scene naturally suggests. 176 — the improper improvements it has suffered. 177 — injudicious manner of opening views. 178 — scenery around Fountain's abbey. 179 — the propriety, and beauty of fragments uniting with a ruin. 180 — description of the ruins of Fountain's abbey. 181 — how restored, and ornamented. 182 — anecdote of Henry Jenkins. 184.

SECT. XXVI.

Hackfall. 187 — description of the scenery there. 187 — vale of Mowbray. 189 — natural idea suggested by the scenes of Hackfall. 190 — remarks on a profusion of buildings in landscape. 190 — comparison between Studley, and Corby. 193 — and between Hackfall, and Persfield. 194 — anecdote of Cromwell. 195 — and of the battle of Marsden-moor. 197.

SECT. XXVII.

Rippon. 199 — Harrowgate. 200 — Harewood-castle, and house. 200 — cursory lights in distant landscape. 200 — country about Leeds, 202 — about Wakefield. 202 — Wentworth-house. 204.

SECT. XXVIII.

General description of the peak of Derbyshire. 207 — description of Middleton-dale. 208 — Hopedale. 209 — rock

— rock at Castleton. 209 — Devil's cave. 210 — Mamtor. 213 — Derbyshire-drop. 213 — Buxton. 214 — Pool's hole. 214 — vale of Ashford. 215 — vale of Haddon; and Haddon-house. 215 — Chatsworth. 216 — Gibbons's carving. 217 — Darley dale. 217 — great Torr. 217 — description of the vale of Matlock. 217.

SECT. XXIX.

Description of Dovedale. 223 — description of Ilam. 228 — Oakover: criticism on Raphael's holy family. 231 — on holy families in general. 232.

SECT. XXX.

Keddleston. 235 — the great hall. 236 — remarks on the entrances of great houses. 237 — pictures at Keddleston. 237 — tower of Derby-church. 239 — china works. 239 — criticism on Raphael's dishes. 239 — silk-mill. 240 — country between Derby, and Leicester. 240 — a fragment of Roman architecture. 241 — Leicester-abbey. 243 — death of Cardinal Wolsey, a good subject for a picture. 244 — anecdote of Richard III. 245.

SECT. XXXI.

Country about Leicester. 247 — cattle considered in a picturesque light. 248 — as single objects. 248 — as combined in groups. 249 — subordination in groups, to be observed as a principle in combination. 255 — Virgil's authority quoted. 256.

SECT.

SECT. XXXII.

Country about Northampton. 259 — Lord Strafford's, and Lord Hallifax's improvements. 259 — beautiful lanes. 260 — Wooburn-abbey. 260 — country about Dunftable. 261 — St. Alban's church. 261 — Verulam. 262 — country about Barnet. 263 — Highgate-hill. 263 — defcription of one of the great avenues into London. 263.

OBSERVATIONS

ON THE

LAKES OF CUMBERLAND, &c.

SECTION XVI.

HAVING refreshed ourselves, and our horses, after a fatiguing morning, we proceeded along the vale of Butermer; and following the course of the river, as far as the inequalities of the ground would admit, we soon came to another lake, still more beautiful, than that we had left above. The two lakes bear a great resemblance to each other. Both are oblong: both wind round promontories; and both are surrounded by mountains. But the lower lake is near a mile longer, than the upper one; the lines it forms are much easier; and tho it has less wood on it's banks, the lofs is compenfated by a richer difplay of rocky fcenery. The forms of thefe rocks are in general, beautiful; moft of them being broken into grand fquare furfaces. This fpecies, as we have already obferved*, are in a greater ftyle, than the cragg, which is fhattered into more diminutive parts.

With this rocky fcenery much hilly ground is intermixed. Patches of meadow alfo, here and there, on the banks of the lake, improve the variety. Nothing is wanting but a little more wood, to make this lake, and the vale in which it lies, a very inchanting fcene; or rather a fucceffion of inchanting fcenes; for the hills, and rifing grounds, into which it every where fwells, acting in due fubordination to the grand mountains, which inviron the whole vale, break and feparate the area of it into fmaller parts. Many of thefe form little vallies, and other recefles, which are very picturefque.

---

* See vol. i. page 108

Not far from this lake the mountain of Grafmer appears rifing above all the mountains in it's neighbourhood. A *lake* of this name we had already feen in our road between Amblefide, and Kefwick; but there is no connection between the *lake,* and the *mountain.*

This mountain forms rather a vaft ridge, than a pointed fummit; and is connected with two or three other mountains of inferior dignity: itfelf is faid to be equal to Skiddaw; which is the common gage of altitude through the whole country; and therefore it may be fuppofed to be the higheft. No mountain afpires to be higher than Skiddaw: fome boaft an equal height: but two or three only have real pretenfions.

Grafmer, and the mountains in it's neighbourhood, form the eaftern boundary of the vale, which we now traverfed; a vale at leaft five miles in length, and one third of that fpace in breadth. Our road carried us near the

the village of Brackenthwait, which lies at the bottom of Grasmer.

Here we had an account of an inundation occasioned by the bursting of a water-spout. The particulars, which are well authenticated, are curious.—In that part, where Grasmer is connected with the other high lands in it's neighbourhood, three little streams take their origin; of which the Lissa is the least inconsiderable. The course of this stream down the mountain is very steep, and about a mile in length. It's bed, and the sides of the mountain all around, are profusely scattered with loose stones, and gravel. On leaving the mountain, the Lissa divides the vale, through which we now passed; and, after a course of four or five miles, falls into the Cocker.

On the 9th of September 1760, about midnight, the water-spout fell upon Grasmer, nearly, as was conjectured, where the three little streams, just mentioned, issue from their fountains.

At firſt it ſwept the whole ſide of the mountain, and charging itſelf with all the rubbiſh it found there, made it's way into the vale, following chiefly the direction of the Liſſa. At the foot of the mountain it was received by a piece of arable ground; on which it's violence firſt broke. Here it tore away trees, ſoil, and gravel; and laid all bare, many feet in depth, to the naked rock. Over the next ten acres it ſeems to have made an immenſe roll; covering them with ſo vaſt a bed of ſtones; that no human art can ever again reſtore the ſoil.

When we ſaw the place, tho twelve years after the event, many marks remained, ſtill flagrant, of this ſcene of ruin. We ſaw the natural bed of the Liſſa, a mere contracted rivulet; and on it's banks the veſtiges of a ſtony channel, ſpreading far and wide, almoſt enough to contain the waters of the Rhine, or the Danube. It was computed from the flood-marks, that in many parts the ſtream muſt have been five or ſix yards deep, and near a hundred broad; and if it's great velocity be added to this weight of water, it's force will be found equal to almoſt any effect.

On the banks of this ſtony channel, we ſaw a few ſcattered houſes, a part of the village of Brackenthwait, which had a wonderful eſcape. They ſtood at the bottom of Graſmer, rather on a riſing ground; and the current, taking it's firſt direction towards them, would have undermined them in a few moments, (for the ſoil was inſtantly laid bare) had not a projection of native rock, the interior ſtratum, on which the houſes had unknowingly been founded, reſiſted the current, and given it a new direction. Unleſs this had intervened, it is probable, the houſes, and all their inhabitants (ſo inſtantaneous was the ruin) had been ſwept away together.

In paſſing farther along the vale, we ſaw other marks of the fury of this inundation; bridges had been thrown down, houſes carried off, and woods rooted up. But it's effects on a ſtone-cauſeway were thought the moſt ſurprizing. This fabric was of great thickneſs, and ſupported on each ſide by an enormous bank of earth. The memory of man could trace it, unaltered in any particular near a hundred years: but by the ſoundneſs and firmneſs of it's parts and texture, it ſeemed as if it had ſtood for ages. It was almoſt a doubt, whether it were a work of nature, or of art. This maſſy mole the deluge not only carried off, but, as if it turned it into ſport, made it's very foundations the channel of it's own ſtream.

Having done all this miſchief, not only here, but in many other parts, the Liſſa threw all it's waters into the Cocker, where an end was put to it's devaſtation: for tho the Cocker was unable to contain ſo immenſe an increaſe; yet as it flows through a more level country, the deluge ſpread far and wide, and waſted it's ſtrength in one vaſt, ſtagnant inundation.

Having paſſed through the vale of Butermer, we entered another beautiful ſcene, the vale of Lorton.

This vale, like all the paſt, preſents us with a landſcape, intirely new. No lakes, no rocks are here, to blend the ideas of dignity, and grandeur with that of beauty. All is ſimplicity, and repoſe. Nature, in this ſcene, lays totally aſide her majeſtic frown, and wears only a lovely ſmile.

The vale of Lorton is of the extended kind, running a confiderable way between mountains, which range at about a mile's diftance. They are near enough to fkreen it from the ftorm, and yet not fo impending as to exclude the fun. Their fides, tho not fmooth, are not much diverfified. A few knolls and hollows juft give a little variety to the broad lights and fhades, which overfpread them.

This vale which enjoys a rich foil, is in general a rural, cultivated fcene; tho in many parts the ground is beautifully broken, and abrupt. A bright ftream, which might almoft take the name of a river, pours along a rocky channel; and fparkles down numberlefs little cafcades. It's banks are adorned with wood; and varied with different objects; a bridge; a mill; a hamlet; a glade over-hung with wood; or fome little fweet recefs; or natural vifta, through which the eye ranges, between irregular trees, along the windings of the ftream.

Except the mountains, nothing in all this fcenery is *great*; but every part is filled with thofe fweet engaging paffages of nature, which
tend

tend to sooth the mind, and instill tranquillity.

> ——— The passions to divine repose
> Persuaded yield; and love and joy alone
> Are waking; love and joy, such as await
> An angel's meditation ———

Scenes of this kind, (however pleasing) in which few objects occur, either of *grandeur* or *peculiarity*, in a singular manner elude the powers of verbal description. They almost elude the power of colours. The soft and elegant form of beauty is hard to hit: while the strong, harsh feature is a mark, which every pencil can strike.

But tho a *peculiar* difficulty attends the verbal description of these mild and quiet haunts of Nature; yet undoubtedly *all* her scenery is ill-attempted in language.

Mountains, rocks, broken-ground, water, and wood, are the simple materials, which she employs in all her beautiful pictures: but the variety and harmony, with which she employs them are infinite. In description these words stand only for *general ideas:* on her charts each is *detailed* into a thousand
varied

varied forms. Words may give the great outlines of a country. They can meafure the dimenfions of a lake. They can hang it's fides with wood. They can rear a caftle on fome projecting rock: or place an ifland near this, or the other fhore. But their range extends no farther. They cannot mark the characteriftic diftinctions of each fcene — the touches of nature — her living tints — her endlefs varieties, both in form and colour. —— In a word, all her elegant *peculiarities* are beyond their reach. Language is equally unable to convey thefe to the eye; as the eye is to convey the various divifions of found to the ear.

The pencil, it is true, offers a more perfect mode of defcription. It fpeaks a language more intelligible; and defcribes the fcene in ftronger and more varied terms. The fhapes, and hues of objects it delineates, and marks, with more exactnefs. It gives the lake the louring fhade of tempeft; or the glowing blufh of fun-fet. It fpreads a warmer, or a colder tint on the tufts of the foreft. It adds form to the caftle; and tips it's fhattered battlements with light. — But all this, all that words can exprefs, or even the pencil defcribe, are grofs, infipid fubftitutes of the living, fcene*. We may be pleafed with the defcription, and the picture: but the foul can *feel* neither, unlefs the force of our own imagination aid the poet's, or the painter's art; exalt the idea, and *picture things unseen.*

Hence it perhaps follows, that the perfection of the art of painting is not fo much attained by an endeavour to form an exact refemblance of nature in a *nice reprefentation of all her minute parts*, which we confider as almoft impracticable, ending generally in flatnefs, and infipidity; as by aiming to give thofe bold, thofe ftrong characteriftic touches which excite the imagination; and lead it to form half the picture itfelf. Painting is the *art of deceiving*; and it's great perfection lies in the exercife of this art.

Hence it is that genius, and an accurate knowledge of nature are as requifite in examining a

---

* This is not at all inconfiftent with what is faid in the 119th page. *Here* we fpeak chiefly of the *detail* of nature's works: *there* of the *compofition*. The nearer we approach the character of nature in every mode of imitation, no doubt the better: yet ftill there are many irregularities and deformities in the natural fcene, which we may wifh to correct—that is, to correct, by improving one part of nature by another.

picture, as in painting one. The cold, untutored eye, tho it may enjoy the *real* scene, (be it history*, landscape, or what it will) is unmoved at the finest *representation*. It does not see an *exact* resemblance of what it sees abroad; and having no *internal pencil*, if I may so speak, to work within; it is utterly unable to *administer* a picture to itself. Whereas the learned eye†, versed equally in nature, and art,

---

* History-painting is certainly the most elevated species. Nothing exalts the human mind so much, as to see the great actions of our fellow-creatures brought before the eye. But this pleasure we seldom find in painting. So much is required from the history-painter, so intimate a knowledge both of nature and art, that we rarely see a history-piece, even from the best masters, that is able to *raise raptures.* We may admire the colouring, or the execution, or some under-part; but the *soul is seldom reached.* The imagination soars beyond the picture —— In the inferior walks of painting, where less is required, more of course is performed: and tho we have few good pictures in history, we have many in portrait, in landscape, in animal-life, dead-game, fruit, and flowers. History-painting is a mode of epic; and tho the literary world abounds with admirable productions in the lower walks of poetry, an epic is the wonder of an age.

† The admirers of painting may be divided into two classes.——The inferior admirer values himself on *distinguishing the master*—on knowing the peculiar touch of each pencil;

art, easily compares the picture with it's archetype: and when it finds the characteristic touches of nature, the imagination immediately takes fire; and glows with a thousand beautiful ideas, *suggested* only by the canvas. When the canvas therefore is so artificially wrought, as to suggest these ideas in the strongest manner, the picture is then most perfect. This is generally best done by little

---

pencil; and the ruling tint of every pallet. But he has no *feeling*. If the picture be an *original*, or if it be in the master's *best manner* (which may be the case of many a bad picture) it is the object of his veneration; tho the story be ill-told: the characters feebly marked, and a total deficiency appear in every excellence of the art.

The more liberal professor, (and who alone is here considered as capable of *administering* a picture to himself) thinks the *knowledge of names*, (any farther than as it marks excellence, till we get a better criterion,) is the bane of the art he admires. A work, worthy of admiration, may be produced by an inferior hand; and a paltry composition may escape from a master. He would have the *intrinsic merit* of a work, not any *arbitrary stamp* proclaim it's excellence. In examining a picture, he leaves the *name* intirely out of the question. It may mislead, it cannot assist, his judgment. The characters of nature, and the knowledge of art, are all he looks for: the rest, be they Michael Angelo's, or Raphael's, he despises as the bubbles of picture-dealers; the mere sweepings, and refuse of Italian garrets.

labour,

labour, and great knowledge. It is knowledge only, which infpires that free, that fearlefs, and determined pencil, fo expreffive in a fkilful hand. As to the *minutiæ* of nature, the picturefque eye will generally fuggeft them better itfelf; and yet give the artift, as he deferves, the credit of the whole.

We fometimes indeed fee pictures *highly finifhed*, and *yet full of fpirit*. They will bear a nice examination at hand, and yet lofe nothing of their diftant effect. But fuch pictures are fo exceedingly rare, that I fhould think, few painters would in prudence attempt a *laboured manner*. Indeed, as pictures are not defigned to be feen through a microfcope, but at a proper diftance, it is labour thrown away*.

Hence it is that even a rough fketch, by the hand of a mafter will often ftrike the imagination beyond the moft finifhed work.

---

* In the higher walks of painting I know of no artift, who does not lofe his fpirit in attempting to finifh highly. In the inferior walks we have a few. Among thefe firft we may rank Van Huyfum, who painted flowers, and fruits, with equal labour and fpirit. And yet even here, I own I have more pleafure in helping myfelf to thefe delicacies from the bolder works of Baptifte.

I have

I have seen the learned eye pass unmoved along rows of pictures by the cold, and inanimate pencil of such a master as Carlo Marat; and start astonished, when it came to a sketch of Rubens. In one case the painter endeavouring in vain to *administer every thing* by giving the full roundness, and smoothness to every part, instead of the bold, characteristic touches of nature, had *done too much:* in the other, tho the work was left unfinished, yet many of the bold *characteristic touches* being thrown in, enough was done to excite the imagination of the spectator, which could easily *supply the rest*.

A very ingenious writer[*] indeed gives another reason for our being better pleased with a sketch, than with a finished piece. *The imagination,* says he, *is entertained with the promise of something more; and does not acquiesce in the present object of the sense.* But this observation, I think, is scarce founded on truth. It is true *the imagination does not acquiesce in the present object of the sense:* but I should suppose, not because it is entertained

---

[*] Burke on the sublime and beautiful, Part ii. Sect. xi.

with a *promife of fomething more*; but becaufe it has the power, of *creating fomething more itfelf*. If *a promife of fomething more*, were the caufe of this pleafure, it fhould feem, that a fketch, in it's rudeft form, would be more pleafing, than when it is more advanced: for the imagination muft have ftill *higher* entertainment in proportion to the *largenefs* of the promife. But this is not the cafe. The fketch, in it's naked chalk-lines, affects us little in comparifon. The inftrument muft be tuned higher, to excite vibrations in the imagination.

Again, on the fame fuppofition, one fhould imagine, that the rude beginning, or rough plan of a houfe, would pleafe us more than the compleat pile; for *the imagination is entertained with the promife of fomething more.* But, I believe, no one was ever fo well pleafed with an unfinifhed fhell, amidft all it's rubbifh of fcaffolding, paper-windows, and other deformities; as with a ftructure compleat in all it's members, and fet off with all it's proper decorations. — But on the fuppofition I have ventured to fuggeft, we fee why the *fketch* may pleafe beyond the *picture*; tho the *unfinifhed fabric* difappoints. An elegant houfe is a

compleat

compleat object. The imagination can rise no higher. It receives full satisfaction. But a picture is *not an object itself*; but only the *representation* of an object. We may easily therefore conceive, that it may fall below it's archetype; and also below the imagination of the spectator, whose fancy may be more picturesque, than the hand of the artist, who composed the picture. In this case, a sketch may afford the spectator more pleasure, as it gives his imagination freer scope; and suffers it to compleat the artist's imperfect draught from the fund of it's own richer, and more perfect ideas.

The variety of scenes, which nature exhibits; and their infinite combinations, and peculiarities, to which neither language, nor colours, unaided by imagination, can, in any degree, do justice; gave occasion to these remarks, which have carried me perhaps too far into digression.

We had to regret, that we saw the vale of Lorton only in half it's beauty. It was at too late an hour; and the evening besides was dark. The morning had been cloudy;

in some part of it rather tempestuous; and we thought ourselves then very happy in the disposition of the weather; for as we had before seen the mountains in a clear atmosphere; it was a desirable variety to see the grand effects they produced in a storm. A mountain is an object of grandeur; and it's dignity receives new force by mixing with the clouds; and arraying itself in the majesty of darkness. Here the idea of *infinity* * produces strongly the sublime. But the chearful scenes of such a vale as this, pretend not to dignity: they are mere scenes of tranquillity. The early ray of dawn, the noon-tide shade, or evening-glow, are the circumstances, in which they most rejoice: a storm, in any shape, will injure them. Here therefore we might have dispensed with more light, and sunshine. Or at the close of the day we might have wished for a quiet, tranquil hour, when the glimmering surfaces of things are sometimes perhaps more pleasing — at all times certainly more soothing, than images of the brightest hue:

---

* See page 228. Vol. 1.

When through the dusk obscurely seen
Sweet evening-objects intervene.

The evening, which grew more tempestuous, began to close upon us, as we left the more beautiful parts of the vale of Lorton. We were still about six miles from Keswick; and had before us a very wild country, which probably would have afforded no great amusement even in full day: but amid the obscurity, which now overspread the landscape, the imagination was left at large; and painted many images, which perhaps did not really exist, upon the dead colouring of nature. Every great and pleasing form, whether clear, or obscure, which we had seen during the day, now played, in strong imagery before the fancy: as when the grand chorus ceases, ideal music vibrates in the ear.

In one part, a view pleased us much; tho perhaps, in stronger light, it might have escaped notice. The road made a sudden dip into a little, winding valley; which being too abrupt for a carriage, was eased by a bridge:

bridge: and the form of the arch was what we commonly find in Roman aqueducts. At least such it appeared to us. The winding road; the woody valley, and broken ground below; the mountain beyond; the form of the bridge, which gave a classic air to the scene, and the obscurity, which melted the whole into one harmonious mass; made all together a very pleasing view.

But it soon grew too dark even for the imagination to roam. It was now ten o'clock; and tho in this northern climate, the twilight of a clear summer-evening affords, even at that late hour, a bright effulgence; yet now all was dark.

—————————— A faint, erroneous ray
Glanced from th' imperfect surfaces of things,
Threw half an image on the straining eye.
While wavering woods, and villages, and streams,
And rocks, and mountain-tops, that long retained
Th' ascending gleam, were all one swimming scene,
Uncertain if beheld ——————

We could just discern, through the dimness of the night, the shadowy forms of the mountains, sometimes blotting out half the
sky,

sky, on one side; and sometimes winding round, as a gloomy barrier on the other.

Often too the road would appear to dive into some dark abyss, a cataract roaring at the bottom: while the mountain-torrents on every side rushed down the hills in notes of various cadence, as their quantities of water, the declivities of their fall, their distances, or the intermission of the blast, brought the sound fuller, or fainter to the ear; which organ became now more alert, as the imagination depended rather on it, than on the eye, for information.

These various notes of water-music, answering each other from hill to hill, were a kind of translation of that passage in the psalms, in which *one deep* is represented *calling another because of the noise of the water-pipes.*

Among other images of the night, a lake (for the lake of Bassenthwait was now in view) appeared through the uncertainty of the gloom, like something of ambiguous texture, spreading a lengthened gleam of wan, dead light under the dark shade of the incumbent mountains: but whether this light were owing to vapours arifing from the valley; or whether it was water — and if water, whether it was an arm of the fea, a lake, or a river — to the uninformed traveller would appear matter of great uncertainty. Whatever it was, it would feem fufficient to alarm his apprehenfions; and to raife in his fancy, (now in queft of dangers,) the idea of fomething, that might ftop his farther progrefs.

A good turnpike-road, on which we entered near the village of Lorton, and a knowledge of the country, fet at nought all fuch ideas with us: but it may eafily be conceived, that a traveller, wandering in the midft of a ftormy night, in a mountainous country, unknown, and unbeaten by human footfteps, might feel palpitations of a very uneafy kind.

We have in Offian fome beautiful images, which accompany a night-ftorm in fuch a country as this. I fhall fubjoin, with a few alterations, an extract from them; as it will illuftrate the fubject before us. It is contained in a note on *Croma*; in which feveral bards are introduced entertaining their patron with their refpective defcriptions of the night.

The

The storm gathers on the tops of the mountains; and spreads it's black mantle before the moon. It comes forward in the majesty of darkness, moving upon the wings of the blast. It sweeps along the vale, and nothing can withstand it's force. The lightning from the rifted cloud flashes before it: the thunder rolls among the mountains in it's rear.

All nature is restless, and uneasy.

The stag lies wakeful on the mountain-moss: the hind close by his side. She hears the storm roaring through the branches of the trees. She starts — and lies down again.

The heath-cock lifts his head at intervals; and returns it under his wing.

The owl leaves her unfinished dirge; and sits ruffled in her feathers in a cleft of the blasted oak.

The famished fox shrinks from the storm, and seeks the shelter of his den.

The hunter alarmed, leaps from his pallet in the lonely hut. He raises his decaying fire. His wet dogs smoke around him. He half-opens his cabin-door, and looks out: but he instantly retreats from the terrors of the night.

For now the whole storm descends. The mountain torrents join their impetuous streams The growing river swells.

The benighted traveller pauses as he enters the gloomy dell. The glaring sky discovers at intervals the terrors of the scene. With a face of wild despair he looks round. He recollects neither the rock above, nor the precipice below. — He stops. — Again he urges his bewildered way. His steed trembles at the frequent flash. The thunder bursts over his head — The torrents roar aloud — He attempts the rapid ford. — Heard you that scream? — It was the shriek of death.

How tumultuous is the bosom of the lake! The waves lash it's rocky side. The boat is brimful in the cove. The oars are dashed against the shore.

What melancholy shade is that sitting under the tree on the lonely beach? — I just discern it faintly shadowed out by the pale beam of the moon, passing through a thin-robed cloud. — It is a female form. — Her eyes are fixed upon the lake. Her hair floats loose around her arm, which supports her pensive head. —— Ah! mournful maid; dost thou

still

still expect thy lover over the lake? — Thou sawest his distant boat, at the close of day, dancing upon the feathery waves. — Thy breast throbs with suspence: but thou knowest not yet, that he lies a corpse upon the shore.

SECT. XVII.

AFTER a wet, and ftormy night we rejoiced to fee the morning arife with all the figns of a calm and fplendid day. We wifhed for the opportunity of furveying Ullefwater in ferene, bright weather. This was the next fcene we propofed to vifit; and with which we intended to clofe our views of this picturefque country.

From Kefwick we mounted a hill, on the great turnpike road to Penrith. At the fummit we left our horfes; and went to examine a Druid temple, in a field on the right. The diameter of this circle is thirty-two *paces*; which, as nearly as could be judged from fo inaccurate a mode of menfuration, is the diameter of Stonehenge; which I once mea-
fured

sured in the same way. But the structures are very different; tho the diameters may be nearly equal. The stones here are diminutive in comparison with those on Salisbury-Plain. If Stonehenge were a cathedral in it's day; this circle was little more than a country church.

These structures, I suppose, are by far the most ancient vestiges of architecture (if we may call them architecture) which we have in England. Their rude workmanship hands down the great barbarity of the times of the Druids: and furnishes strong proof of the savage nature of the religion of these heathen priests. Within these magical circles we may conceive any incantations to have been performed; and any rites of superstition to have been celebrated. It is history, as well as poetry, when Ossian mentions the *circles of stones*, where our ancestors, in their nocturnal orgies, invoked the spirits which rode upon the winds — the awful forms of their deceased forefathers; through which, he sublimely tells us, *the stars dimly twinkled*.

As fingular a part as the Druids make in the ancient hiftory, not only of Britain, but of other countries, I know not, that I ever faw any of their tranfactions introduced as the fubject of a capital picture. That they can furnifh a fund of excellent imagery for poetry we know: and I fee not why the fcenes of Caractacus might not be as well fuited to picturefque, as dramatic repiefentation. — And yet there is a difference. The drama depends at leaft as much on fentiment, as on reprefentation. Whereas the picture depends intirely on the latter. The beautiful fentiments of the poet are loft; and the fpectator muft make out the dialogue, as he is able, from the energetic looks of the figures. — Hence therefore it follows, that the fame fubjects are not equally calculated to fhine in poetry, and in painting.

Thofe fubjects, no doubt, are beft adapted to the pencil, which *unfold themfelves by action*. In general, however, all animated ftories, which admit either of *ftrong action*, or *paffion*, are judicioufly chofen. Unanimated fubjects have little chance of producing an effect; particularly

cularly love-stories; which, of all others, I could wish to exclude from canvas. The language of love is so difficult to translate, that I know not that I ever saw a *representation* of lovers, who were not strongly marked with the character of simpletons.

But besides such subjects, as admit of strong *action*, or *passion*, there are others of a more *inanimate* cast, which, through the *peculiarity* of the characters, of which they consist, can never be mistaken. Such is the settlement of Pensylvania, painted by Mr. West. From the mixture of English, and Indian characters, and a variety of apposite appendages, the story is not only well told; but, as every picturesque story should be told, it is obvious at sight.

Among subjects of this kind, are those, which occasioned this digression — druidical subjects. I know few of the *less animated kind*, which would admit more picturesque embellishment, than a Druid-sacrifice. The peculiar character, and savage features of these barbarous priests — their white flowing vestments — the branch of misleto, which they hold — the circular stones (if they could be brought into composition) — the spreading oak
— the

— the altar beneath it — and the milk-white steer — might all together form a good picture.

I have often admired an etching by Teipolo, which I have always conceived to be a reprefentation of this fubject.* He does not indeed introduce all the circumftances of a Druid-facrifice, which I have here enumerated: but the characters are fuch, as exactly fuit the fubject; and the whole feems to be an excellent illuftration of it.

After we left the temple of the Druids, we met with little which engaged our attention, till we came to the *vale of St. John.* This fcene appeared from the ftand, where we viewed it, to be a circular area, of about fix, or feven miles in circumference. It is furrounded intirely by mountains; and is watered by a fmall river, called the Giata.

The vale of St. John is efteemed one of the moft celebrated fcenes of beauty in the coun-

---

* It is contained in a book of etchings on emblematical fubjects.

try: but it did not anfwer our expectation. The ground, confifting of patches of fenced meadow, adorned with farm-houfes, and clumps of trees, was beautifully tumbled about in many parts: but the whole was rather rich, than picturefque: and on this account, I fuppofe, it hath obtained it's celebrity. It's circular form alfo, every where within the fcope of the eye, wanted that variety, which the *winding* vale affords; where one part is continually receding from another in all the pleafing gradations of perfpective.*

The *kind* of fcenery here, is much the fame, as in the vale of Lorton: both are compofed of rural objects, but thefe objects are differently prefented. In the vale of Lorton, the houfes, and hamlets, feated on a wandering ftream, are confined to the fame level; and appear of courfe, *one after another*, as fo many little *feparate landfcapes*. Here they are fcattered about the inequalities of the ground, through the area of a vale, circular at leaft in appearance, and offer the eye *too much at once* — a *confufion*, rather than a *fuc-*

---

* See the fame idea applied to water, page 184. Vol. i.

ceffion,

ceſſion, of ſcenery. I ſpeak however only of the *general appearance* of the vale : it contains undoubtedly many beautiful ſcenes, if we had had time to explore them.

The plan, or ground-plot, of the vale of Tempe, as we have it deſcribed by ancient authors, was ſomewhat ſimilar to this of St. John. Nature ſeems in both to have wrought on the ſame model; excepting only that the furniture of that very celebrated ſcene of antiquity was probably more picturesque.

The vale of Tempe, like this, was circular, and incompaſſed with mountains. It's area was compoſed of lawns, interſperſed with wood; which in many parts was thick, and cloſe; and muſt every where have intercepted ſome portion of the mountain-line, and broken the regularity of a circular *ſhape*.

The mountains too in Tempe were of a more beautiful ſtructure; abrupt, hung with rock, and adorned with wood. — At the head of the vale was a grand, rocky chaſm, ſhaded with a profuſion of woody ſcenery; through which the whole weight of the river Peneus forced it's way, with a tremendous found: and having been dafhed into foam and vapours by the fall, reunited it's ftrength at the bottom, and poured through the vale in a wild, impetuous torrent, roaring over rocks and fhelves, till it found an exit, through the folding of the mountains on the oppofite fide.

Elian indeed tells us, that the ftream was fmooth: but as Ovid's defcription is more picturefque, the reader will give me leave to confider his authority as more decifive. His view of Tempe is very noble: but as he meant principally to defcribe the palace of a river-god, which lay among the caverns, and receffes of the rocky chafm at the entrance of the vale, his fubject naturally led him to dwell chiefly on the cafcade, which was undoubtedly the greateft ornament of the place.

> Eft nemus Æmoniæ, prærupta quod undique claudit
> Silva. vocant Tempe: per quæ Peneus ab imo
> Effufus Pindo, fpumofis volvitur undis;
> Dejectuque gravi tenues agitantia fumos
> Nubila conducit; fummafque afpergine filvas
> Impluit: & fonitu plus quam vicina fatigat.
> Hæc domus, hæ fedes, hæc funt penetralia magni
> Amnis: in hoc refidens facto de cautibus antro,
> Undis jura dabat ⸺

A vale

A vale thus circumstanced is so pleasing, that other poets have seized the idea in their descriptions. I could multiply quotations: but I shall select two, in which the same subject is treated in a different manner. In one the natural grandeur of the scene is softened by little circumstances of chearfulness: in the other, it strikes in the full majesty of the sublime. The former is more the vale of St. John: the latter approaches nearer the idea of the Thessalian vale.

>Into a forest far they thence him led,
>Where was their dwelling in a pleasant glade,
>With mountains round about invironed.
>And mighty woods that did the valley shade,
>And like a stately theatre it made,
>Spreading itself into a spacious plain.
>And in the midst a little river played
>Amongst the pumy stones, which seemed to plain,
>With gentle murmur that his course they did restrain.

>——————————— The hills
>Of Æta, yielding to a fruitful vale,
>Within their range half-circling had inclosed
>A fair expanse in verdure smooth. The bounds
>Were edged by wood, o'erhung by hoary cliffs,
>Which from the clouds bent frowning. Down a rock,
>Above the loftiest summit of the grove,

A tumbling torrent wore the shagged stone;
Then gleaming through the intervals of shade,
Attained the valley, where the level stream
Diffused refreshment ————

The vale of St. John was, some years ago, the scene of one of those terrible inundations, which wasted lately the vale of Brackenthwait. I shall relate the circumstances of it, as they were given us on the spot: but as we had them not perhaps on the best authority, they may, in some particulars, be overcharged.

It was on the 22d of August 1749, that this disaster happened. That day, which had been preceded by weather uncommonly close and sultry, set in with a gloomy aspect. The blackness gathered, more, and more, from every quarter. The air was hot beyond sufferance. The whole atmosphere glowed, and every thing around was in a state of perfect stagnation. Not a leaf was in motion.

In the mean time, the inhabitants of the vale heard a strange noise in various parts around them: but whether it was in the air, or whether it arose from the mountains, they could not ascertain. It was like the hollow
murmur

murmur of a rising wind, among the tops of trees. This noise (which in a smaller degree is not an uncommon prelude to a storm) continued without intermission about two hours, when a tempest of wind, and rain, and thunder, and lightning succeeded, which was violent, beyond any thing, remembered in former times; and lasted, without pause, near three hours.

During this storm the cataract fell upon the mountain, on the north of the vale, or as some people thought, tho I should suppose without any probability, burst from the bowels of it. The side of that mountain is a continued precipice, through the space of a mile. This whole tract, we were told, was covered in an instant, with one continuous cascade of roaring torrent (an appearance which must have equalled the fall of Niagara) sweeping all before it from the top of the mountain to the bottom. There, like that other inundation, it followed the channel of the brooks it met with; and shewed similar effects of it's fury.

One of these effects was astonishing. The fragments of rock, and deluges of stone, and sand, which were swept from the mountain by the torrent, choked one of the streams, which received it at the bottom. The water, thus pent up, and receiving continually vast accession of strength, after rolling sullenly about that part of the vale in frightful whirl-pools, at length forced a new channel through a solid rock, which we were informed, it disjointed in some fractured crevice, and made a chasm at least ten feet wide. Many of the fragments were carried to a great distance; and some of them were so large, that a dozen horses could not move them. We were sorry afterwards, that we had not seen this remarkable chasm: but we had not time to go in quest of it.

From the vale of St. John we ascended a steep hill, called Branthwait-cragg; where being obliged to leave the great road in our way to Ullefwater, and investigate a pathless desert over the mountains, which invironed us; we put ourselves under the conduct of a guide.

These mountains were covered with a profusion of huge stones, and detached rocks; among which we found many old people, and

and children, from the neighbouring villages, gathering a species of white lychen, that grows upon the craggs; and which we heard had been found very useful in dying a murray-colour.

Among the difficulties of our rout over these mountains, the bogs and morasses we met with, were the most troublesome. We were often obliged to dismount; and in some parts the surface could hardly bear a man. Where rushes grew, our guide informed us, the ground was firmest. We endeavoured therefore, as much as possible, to make the little tussocks of these plants the basis of our footsteps. But as we could not convey this intelligence to our horses, they often plunged very deep.

In several parts of our ride, we had a view of that grand cluster of mountains, which forms a circle in the heart of Cumberland; and makes a back-ground to the views in almost every part of the extremities of that county. These mountains unite on the south with those of Westmoreland. The side next us was composed of Skiddaw.—Threlkate-fell,

fell, a part of which is called Saddle-back — and Grifedale-fell. As we rode nearer the northern limit of this chain, Skiddaw, which is by much the higheſt mountain, appeared in perſpective, the leaſt. Behind theſe mountains ariſe, in order, Moſedale-fell — Carric — and Caudbeck — the tops of which we ſometimes ſaw, from the higher grounds, peering, in their blue attire, over the concave parts of the browner mountains, which ſtood nearer the eye.

Between us, and this circular chain, which occupied the whole horizon on the left, was ſpread a very extenſive vale; ſtretching from ſide to ſide hardly leſs than ſeven or eight miles; and in length winding out of ſight. It affords little beauty, except what ariſes from the gradation of diſtance: but it ſuggeſts an idea of greatneſs, which ſpace, and grand boundaries, however unadorned, will always ſuggeſt.

This idea hath ſometimes miſled the taſteleſs improver of little ſcenes. He has heard, that *ſpace gives beauty*; but not knowing how to accommodate the rule to circumſtances, he

often

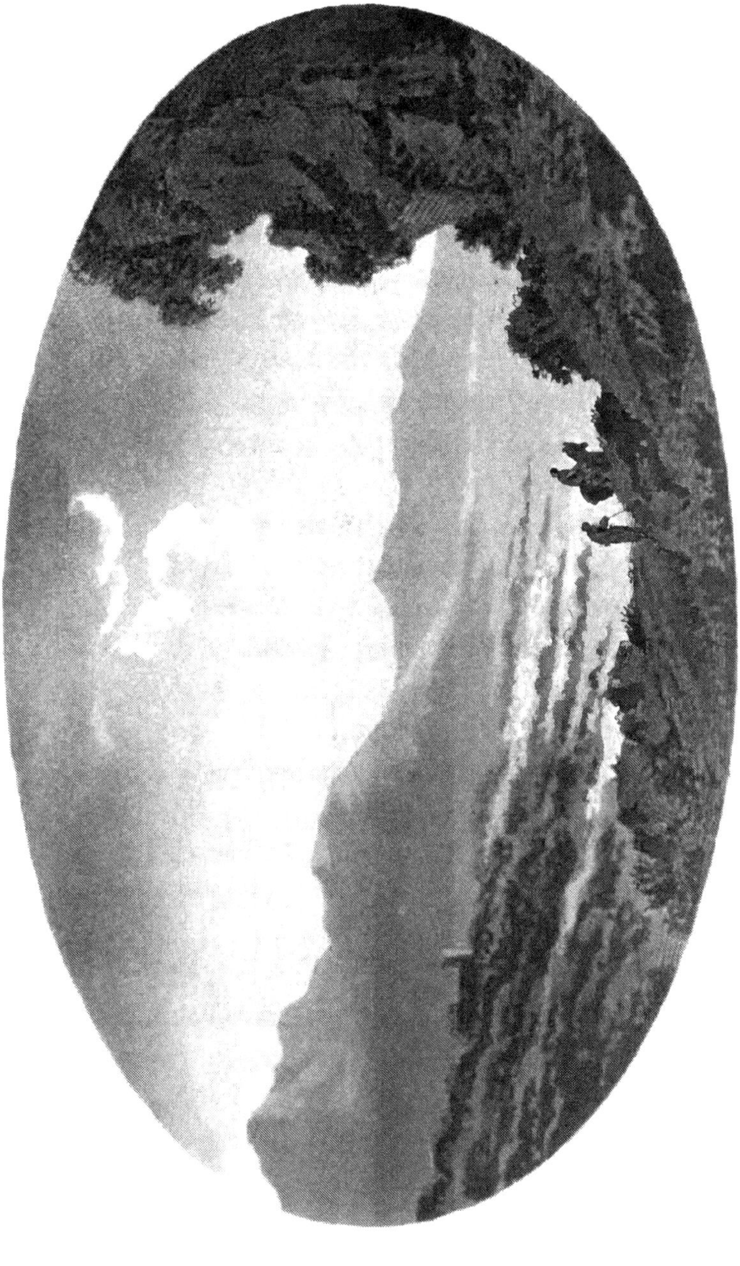

often shews all that is to be seen; when, in fact, he should have hid half of it, as a deformity. *Mere* space gives the idea of *grandeur*, rather than of *beauty*. Such an idea the ocean presents. But a *little* scene cannot present it. *Grandeur* therefore is not attained by attempting it, while *beauty* is often lost.

Along this vale ran the great road we had just left; which was no little ornament to it. The mazy course of a river is a still nobler object of the same kind: but a great road is no bad substitute; and is in some respects superior. The *river* being on a level, and contained within banks, is generally too much hid, unless it be viewed from an elevated point. But the *road* following the inequalities of the ground, is easily traced by the eye, as it winds along the several elevations, and depressions it meets with; and has therefore more variety in it's course.

On the right, forming the other side of this extensive vale, arise several very high moun-

mountains; among which Hara-fide, and White-pike are the moft magnificent. At the bottom of thefe, verging towards the fkirts of the vale, are other hills lefs formidable: but two of them, called the Mell-fells, are very remarkable; being fhaped like earthen graves, in a country church-yard.

A little before we approached the Mell-fells, the path we purfued led us under a towering rocky hill, which is known by the name of *Wolf's-cragg*, and is probably one of the monuments of this animal in Britain. It is a fortrefs intirely adapted to a garrifon of wolves, from whence they might plunder the vale which was fpread before them: and make prey of every thing, as far as the eye could reach. Such a landfcape, in painting, would be highly characterized by fuch appendages. It would have pleafed Ridinger. If that picturefque naturalift had been in queft of a wolf-fcene, he could not have found a better.

When

When we had paffed this range of mountains, we got more into a beaten path, leading to the village of Matterdale, about a mile only from Ullefwater; which was ftill intirely excluded from our fight by high grounds. Here we difmiffed our guide, and were directed into Gobray-park, which is the northern boundary of the lake.

This part of the country we found well inhabited: and the roads, at this feafon, much frequented. It was about the time of a ftatute-fair; when the young people of the feveral villages leave their old fervices, and go to their new: and we were not a little entertained with the fimplicity, and variety of the different groups and figures we met, both on horfeback, and on foot.

Thefe are the picturefque inhabitants of a landfcape. The dreffed-out figures, and gaudy carriages, along the great roads of the capital, afford them not. The pencil rejects with indignation the fplendor of art. In grand fcenes, even the peafant cannot be admitted,
if

if he be employed in the low occupations of his profeſſion: the ſpade, the ſcythe, and the rake are all excluded.

Moral, and picturesque ideas do not always coincide. In a moral light, cultivation, in all its parts, is pleaſing; the hedge, and the furrow; the waving corn field, and rows of ripened ſheaves. But all theſe, the picturesque eye, in queſt of ſcenes of grandeur, and beauty, looks at with diſguſt. It ranges after nature, untamed by art, and burſting wildly into all its irregular forms.

––––––––––––––––––––– Juvat arva videre
Non raſtris hominum, non ulli obnoxia curæ.

It is thus alſo in the introduction of figures. In a moral view, the induſtrious mechanic is a more pleaſing object, than the loitering peaſant. But in a picturesque light, it is otherwiſe. The arts of induſtry are rejected; and even idleneſs, if I may ſo ſpeak, adds dignity to a character. Thus the lazy cowherd reſting on his pole; or the peaſant lolling on a rock, may be allowed in the grandeſt ſcenes; while the laborious mechanic, with his implements of labour, would be repulſed.

The

The fisherman, it is true, may follow his calling upon the lake: but he is indebted for this privilege, not to his art; but to the picturesque apparatus of it — his boat, and his nets, which qualify his art. *They* are the objects: *he* is but an appendage. Place him on the shore, as a single figure, with his rod, and line; and his art would ruin him. In a chearful glade, along a purling brook, near some mill, or cottage, let him angle, if he please: in such a scene the picturesque eye takes no offence. But let him take care not to introduce the vulgarity of his employment in a scene of grandeur.

At the same time, we must observe, that figures, which thus take their importance merely from not mixing with low, mechanic arts, are at best only *picturesque appendages*. They are of a negative nature, neither adding to the grandeur of the idea, nor taking from it. They merely and simply *adorn* a scene.

The characters, which are most *suited to these scenes* of grandeur, are such as impress us with some idea of greatness, wildness, or ferocity; all which touch on the sublime.

Figures

Figures in long, folding draperies; gypfies; banditti; and foldiers, — not in modern regimentals; but as Virgil paints them,

——— longis adnixi haftis, et fcuta tenentes:

are all marked with one or other of thefe characters: and mixing with the magnificence, wildnefs, or horror of the place, they properly coalefce; and reflecting the fame images, add a deeper tinge to the character of the fcene.

For the truth of all thefe remarks I might appeal to the decifive judgment of Salvator Rofa; who feems to have thoroughly ftudied propriety in figures, efpecially in fcenes of grandeur. His works are a model on this head. We have a book of figures, particularly compofed for fcenery of this kind, and etched by himfelf. In this collection there is great variety, both in the characters, groups, and dreffes: but I do not remember, either there, or in any other of his works, a low, mechanic character. All his figures are either of (what I have called) the *negative* kind; or marked with fome trait of *greatnefs*, *wildnefs*, or *ferocity*. Of this laft fpecies his figures
gene-

generally partook: his grand scenes being inhabited chiefly by banditti.

I met with a passage, not a little illustrative of these remarks on figures, in the travels of Mr. Thickness through Spain.

"The worst sort of beggars, says he in Spain are the troops of male, and female gypsies. They are of the genuine breed, and differ widely from all other gypsies; and I may say, from all other human beings. I often met troops of these people; and when an interview happens in roads very distant from towns, or dwellings, it is not very pleasing: for they ask, as if they knew they were not to be refused; and I dare say often commit murders, when they can commit them by surprize. They are extremely swarthy, with hair as black as jet, and form very picturesque groups under the shade of the rocks and trees of the Pyrænean mountains, where they spend their evenings, and live suitably to the climate; where bread, and water, and idleness, are preferable to better fare and hard-labour."

SECT.

SECT. XVIII.

ON defcending the hill from Matterdale, before we came to the lake, we had a beautiful *fpecimen* (as the naturalifts fpeak) of what in this country is called a *gill*. The road carried us along the edge of one of it's precipices: but the chafm was fo intirely filled with wood, that when we looked down, we could not fee into it. Even the fun-beams, unable to enter, refted only on the tufted foliage of the trees, which grew from the fides. — But tho the eye was excluded, the ear was foothed by the harmony of an invifible torrent; whofe notes, founding along innumerable broken falls, and foftened by afcending through the trees, were very melodious.

A winding road brought us to the bottom; where the torrent tumbling out of the wood, received us. We had a ſhort view into the deep receſſes of the ſcene, through the branches of the trees, which ſtretched over the ſtream; but we had not time to penetrate it's alluring ſhade.

Having paſſed over more high grounds, we came at length in view of the lake. The firſt catch of it was thus preſented.

A road occupied the neareſt part of the landſcape, winding around a broken cliff; which roſe conſiderably on the left. A portion of a diſtant mountain appeared on the right, with a ſmall part of the lake at it's foot. The compoſition, as far as it went, was correct: but we yet ſaw only enough to excite our curioſity; and to give us, from the bearing of the land, a general idea of the lake.

Ullefwater is the largeſt lake in this country, except Windermere; being eight miles long; and about two broad in the wideſt part; tho, in general, it rarely exceeds a mile in breadth.

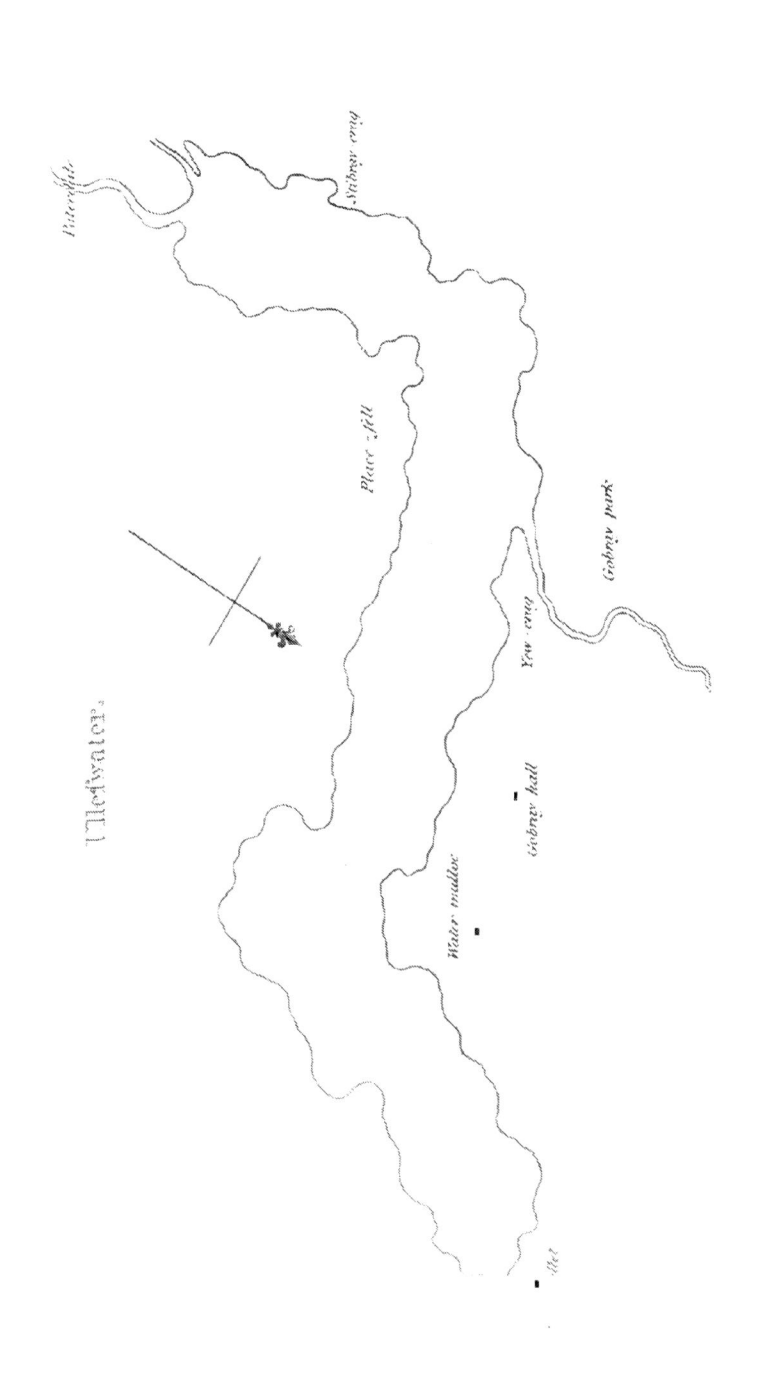

breadth. It points nearly north, and south; as most of these lakes do; but being placed at an *extremity* of the barrier-mountains, it affords a greater variety than is exhibited by such lakes, as are *invironed* by them. These having few accompaniments, receive their character chiefly from the surrounding desolation. Such a lake is Wyburn. Windermere, on the other hand, Keswick, Butermer, and Ullesswater may all be called *boundary-lakes*. One end of each participates more of the rugged country; and the other of the cultivated: tho each end participates, in some degree, of both. A few traits of romantic scenery are added to the tameness of one end; while the native horror of the other is softened by a few chearful appendages.

The form of Ulleswater resembles a Z; only there is no angular acuteness in it's line. It spreads every where in an easy curve; beautifully broken in some parts by promontories. — The middle reach contains in length near two thirds of the lake. The southern side is mountainous; and becomes more so, as it verges towards the west. As the mountains approach the north, they glide (as we have seen is usual in *boundary-lakes*) into meadows and paftures. The northern and weftern fides contain a great variety of woody and rocky fcenes; but thefe alfo, as they approach the eaft, become fmooth and fertilized. At the fouthern point, under impending mountains, lies the village of Patterdale. — With this general idea of Ullefwater, let us return to the defcent from Matterdale, where we caught the firft view of it.

As we defcended a little farther, the whole fcene of the lake opened before us; and fuch a fcene, as almoft drew from us the apoftrophe of the inraptured bard,

> Vifions of glory, fpare my aching fight!

Among all the *vifions* of this inchanting country, we had feen nothing fo beautifully fublime, fo correctly picturefque as this. — And yet I am averfe to make comparifons; efpecially on feeing a country but once. Much depends on the circumftances of light, and weather. I would wifh therefore only to fay, that I was *more pleafed* with Ullefwater, than with any lake I had feen; adding, at the fame time, that we were fortunate in a concurrence of incidents, that aided it's beauty. We had hitherto feen all the lakes we had vifited, under a rough, or cloudy fky: and thó their dignity was certainly increafed by that circumftance; yet the beauty of a lake in fplendid, ferene weather, aided, at this time, by the powers of contraft, made a wonderful impreffion on the imagination. The impreffion might have been the fame, if Ullefwater had been the firft lake, we had feen in a ftorm.

" The effect of the *fublime*, fays Mr. Burke, is *aftonifhment*; and the effect of *beauty*, is *pleafure*: but when the two ingredients mix, the effect is in a good meafure deftroyed in both. They conftitute a fpecies fomething different both from the fublime and beautiful, which I have before called *fine*: but this kind, I imagine, has not fuch a power on the paffions, either as vaft bodies have, which are endowed with the correfpondent qualities of the fublime; or as the qualities of beauty have, when united in a fmall object. The affection produced by large bodies, adorned with the fpoils of beauty, is a tention continually relieved; which approaches to the nature of mediocrity *."

This refined reasoning does not seem intirely grounded on experience. — I do not remember any scene in which beauty and sublimity, according to my ideas, are more blended than in this: and tho Mr. Burke's ideas of beauty are perhaps more exceptionable, than his ideas of the sublime; yet it happens, that most of the qualities, which he predicates of both, unite in this scene. Their effect therefore, according to his argument, should be destroyed. But the feelings of every lover of nature, on viewing these scenes, I dare say, would revolt from such reasoning. Ours certainly did.

The foreground of the grand view before us, is a part of Gobray-park, which belongs to the duke of Norfolk: rough, broken, and woody. Among the old oaks, which inriched it, herds of deer, and cattle grazed in groups. Beyond this is spread an extensive reach of the lake, winding round a rocky promontory on the left;

---

* Sublime and Beautiful, Part IV. Sect. 25.

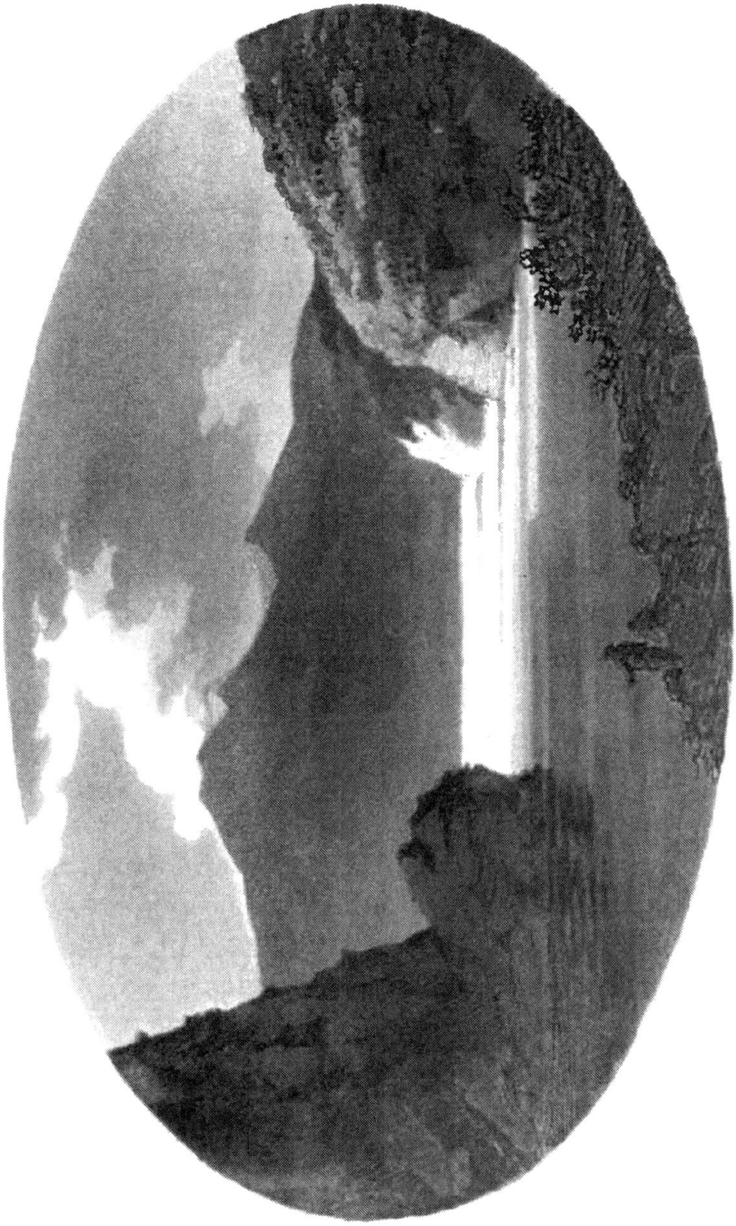

which is the point of a mountain, called Martindale-fell, or Place-fell: the southern boundary of the lake. This promontory uniting with the mountain, lets it easily down into the water, as by a step. An *hesitation*, if I may so call it, of this kind, eases greatly the heaviness of a line. In a *distance*, it is of less consequence: but in all the *nearer* grounds, it is necessary. I speak chiefly however of those views, in which beauty, and grandeur are combined. In those of simple grandeur, and sublimity, as in that of Penmanmaur, for instance, in North Wales, the heavy line, which is very remarkable in that scene, from the Irish road, perhaps strengthens the effect.

Martindale-fell is entirely unplanted; but it's line, and surface are both well varied. Numberless breaks (little vallies, and knolls) give it a lightness, without injuring it's simplicity.

Such was the disposition of the objects, on the left of the lake: on the right, two woody promontories, pursuing each other in perspective, made a beautiful contrast with the smooth continuity of Martindale-fell.

In front, the distance was composed of mountains, falling gently into the lake; near the edge of which lies the village of Patterdale.

We took this view at a point, which had juſt ſo much elevation, as to give a variety to the lines of the lake. As we deſcended to the water, the view was ſtill grand, and beautiful, but had loſt ſome of it's more picturesque beauties: it had loſt the foreground: it had loſt the ſweeping line round the mountain on the left: and it had loſt the receſs between the two woody promontories on the right. The whole margin of the lake was nearly reduced to one ſtraight line. — The beauty of a view, eſpecially in lake-ſcenery, we have before obſerved*, depends greatly on the nice poſition of it's point.

Having ſpent ſome time in examining this very inchanting ſcene, we ſkirted the lake towards Patterdale, on a tolerable road, which runs from one end of it to the other: on the ſouth it is continued to Ambleſide; on the north, to Penrith. I call it a tolerable road; but I mean only for horſes. It has not the

---

* See page 96. vol. i.

quartering

quartering and commodious width of a carriage-road.

As we left Gobray-park, we took our rout along the margin of the firſt of thoſe woody promontories on the right. We were carried by the ſide of the lake, through cloſe lanes, and thick groves: yet not ſo thick, but that we had every where, through the openings of the trees, and windings of the road, views in front, and on the right, into woody receſſes, ſome of which were very pleaſing: and on the left, the lake, and all it's diſtant furniture, broke frequently upon us.

After ſkirting the firſt woody promontory, which carried us about a mile, the road turned ſuddenly to the right, and led us round into the ſecond, riſing a conſiderable height above the water. — In this promontory, a new ſcene opened: the woods became intermixed with rock; and a great variety of beautiful foregrounds were produced. The rocks, through which the road was ſometimes cut, were chiefly on our right. — In this promontory alſo,

as

as well as in the other, we were amufed with catches of the lake, and of Martindale-fell, through the trees.

Scenes, like thefe, are adapted to every ftate of the fky. They were beautiful in the calm feafon, in which we faw them; and in which indeed we wifhed to fee them. But they would have received peculiar advantages alfo from a ftorm. The objects are all in that great ftyle, which is fuited to the violences of nature. The imagination would have rifen with the tempeft, and given a double grandeur to every awful form. — The trees, in the mean time, which rear themfelves ftage above ftage, upon the mountain's brow, and fpread down to the very road, would have made a noble inftrument for the hollow blaft to found, confifting of various notes: while the furges of the lake, refounding among the caverns, and dafhing againft the rocks, many fathoms below, would have aided the concert with new notes of terrific harmony.

──────────────── There is a mood,
(I sing not to the vacant and the young)
There is a kindly mood of melancholy,
That wings the soul, and points her to the sky.
While winds, and tempests sweep the various lyre,
How sweet the diapason! ────────

The mind is not always indeed in unison with such scenes, and circumstances, as these. When it does not happen to be so, no effect can be produced. Sometimes indeed the scene may draw the mind into unison; if it be not under the impression of any strong passion of an opposite kind; but in a sort of neutral state. The effect however will always be strongest, when the mind happens to be possessed of ideas congenial to the scene — when, in a *kindly mood of melancholy*, it feels itself soothed by the objects around.

But besides the music of winds and tempests, the ecchoes, which are excited in different parts of this lake, are still more grand, and affecting. More or less they accompany all lakes, that are circumscribed by lofty, and rocky skreens. We found them on Windermere; we found them on Derwentwater. But
every

every lake, being furrounded by rocks and mountains of a ftructure peculiar to itfelf, forms a variety of inftruments; and, of courfe, a variety of founds. The ecchoes therefore of no two lakes are alike; unlefs they are mere monotonifts

We took notice of a very grand eccho on the weftern fhores of the great ifland in Windermere: but the moft celebrated ecchoes are faid to be found on Ullefwater; in fome of which the found of a cannon is diftinctly reverberated fix, or feven times. It firft rolls over the head in one vaft peal. — Then fubfiding a few feconds, it rifes again in a grand, interrupted burft, perhaps on the right. — Another folemn paufe enfues. Then the found arifes again on the left. — Thus thrown from rock to rock, in a fort of aerial perfpective, it is caught again perhaps by fome nearer promontory, and returning full on the ear, furprizes you, after you thought all had been over, with as great a peal as at firft.

But the grandeft effect of this kind is produced by a *fucceffive* difcharge of cannon*;

---

* The duke of Portland, who has property in this neighbourhood, has a veffel on the lake, with brafs guns, for the purpofe of exciting ecchoes.

at

at the interval of a few feconds between each difcharge. The effect of the firft is not over, when the ecchoes of the fecond, the third, or perhaps of the fourth, begin. Such a variety of awful founds, mixing, and commixing, and at the fame moment heard from all fides, have a wonderful effect on the mind; as if the very foundations of every rock on the lake were giving way; and the whole fcene, from fome ftrange convulfion, were falling, into general ruin.

Thefe founds, which are all of the terrific kind, are fuited chiefly to fcenes of grandeur during fome moment of wildnefs, when the lake is under the agitation of a ftorm. In a calm, ftill evening, the gradations of an eccho, dying away in diftant thunder, are certainly heard with moft advantage. But that is a different idea. You attend then only to the *ecchoes* themfelves. When you take the *fcene* into the combination; and attend to the effect of the *whole together*; no doubt fuch founds, as are of the moft violent kind, are beft fuited to moments of the greateft uproar.

But there is another fpecies of ecchoes, which are as well adapted to the lake in all it's ftillnefs, and tranquillity, as the others

are

are to it's wildnefs, and confufion: and which recommend themfelves chiefly to thofe feelings, which depend on the gentler movements of the mind. Inftead of cannon, let a few French-horns, and clarionets be introduced. Softer mufic than fuch loud wind-inftruments, would fcarce have power to vibrate. The effect is now wonderfully changed. The found of a cannon is heard in burfts. It is the modified mufic of thunder. But the *continuation* of *mufical founds* forms a *continuation* of *mufical ecchoes*; which reverberating around the lake, are exquifitely melodious in their feveral gradations; and form a thoufand fymphonies, playing together from every part. The variety of notes is inconceivable. The ear is not equal to their innumerable combinations. It liftens to a fymphony dying away at a diftance; when other melodious founds arife clofe at hand. Thefe have fcarce attracted the attention; when a different mode of harmony arifes from another quarter. In fhort, every rock is vocal, and the whole lake is transformed into a kind of magical fcene; in which every promontory feems peopled by aerial beings, anfwering each other in celeftial mufic.

——— How

―――――― How often from the steep
Of ecchoing hill, or thicket, have we heard
Celestial voices to the midnight air,
Sole, or responsive each to other's note,
Singing their great Creator? Oft in bands
While they keep watch, or nightly rounding walk,
With heavenly touch of instrumental sounds,
In full harmonic number joined, their songs
Divide the night, and lift our thoughts to heaven.

Having now almost skirted the two woody promontories in our rout to Patterdale, we found the conclusion, the grandest part of the whole scenery. It is a bold projection of rock finely marked, and adorned with hanging woods; under the beetling summit of which the road makes a sudden turn. This is the point of the second promontory; and, I believe, is known by the name of *Stibra-cragg*.

The trees which compose the whole scenery through both these promontories, are in general, oak.

From hence through lanes of the same kind, though less superbly decorated, we came to the village of Patterdale; situated on rising ground, among two or three little rivers,

rivers, or branches of a river, which feed the lake. It lies in a cove of mountains, open in front to the southern reach of the lake; beyond which appear the high, woody lands of Gobray-park. The situation is magnificent.

Among the cottages of this village, stands a house, belonging to a person of somewhat better condition; whose little estate, which he occupies himself, lies in the neighbourhood. As his property, inconsiderable as it is, is better than that of any of his neighbours, it has gained him the title of *King of Patterdale*, in which his family name is lost. His ancestors have long enjoyed the title before him. We had the honour of seeing this prince, as he took the diversion of fishing on the lake; and I could not help thinking, that if I were inclined to envy the situation of any potentate in Europe, it would be that of the king of Patterdale. The pride of Windsor and Versailles would shrink in a comparison with the magnificence of his dominions.

The great fimplicity of this country, and that rigid temperance, and economy, to which neceffity obliges all its inhabitants, may be exemplified by the following little hiftory.

A clergyman, of the name of Mattifon, was minifter of this place fixty years; and died lately at the age of ninety. During the early part of his life, his benefice brought him in only twelve pounds a year. It was afterwards increafed, (I fuppofe by the queen's bounty,) to eighteen; which it never exceeded. On this income he married — brought up four children — lived comfortably among his neighbours — educated a fon, I believe, at the univerfity — and left upwards of one thoufand pounds to his family. — With that fingular fimplicity, and inattention to forms, which characterize a country like this; he himfelf read the burial-fervice over his mother; he married his father to a fecond wife; and afterwards buried him. He publifhed his own banns of marriage in the church, with a woman, whom he had formerly chriftened; and himfelf married all his four children.

From this specimen, the manners of the country may easily be conceived. At a distance from the refinements of the age, they are at a distance also from its vices. Many sage writers, and Montesquieu* in particular, have supposed these rough scenes of nature to have a great effect on the human mind: and have found virtues in mountainous countries, which were not the growth of tamer regions. Many opinions perhaps have passed current among mankind, with less foundation in truth. Montesquieu is in quest chiefly of political virtue — liberty — bravery — and the arts of bold defence: but, I believe, here likewise private virtue is equally befriended. It is the happiness of the people of this rough country, that they have no great roads among them: and that their simple villages, on the sides of lakes, and mountains, are in no line of communication with any of the busy haunts of men. Ignorance is sometimes called the mother of vice. I apprehend it to be as often the nurse of innocence.

---

* Book XVIII. Ch. II.

Much have thofe travellers to anfwer for, whofe cafual intercourfe with this innocent, and fimple people tends to corrupt them; to difleminate among them ideas of extravagance, and diffipation — to give them a tafte for pleafures, and gratifications, of which they had no ideas — to infpire them with difcontent at home — and taint their rough, induftrious manners with idlenefs, and a thirft after difhoneft means.

If travellers would frequent this country with a view to examine it's grandeur, and beauty — or to explore it's varied, and curious regions with the eye of philofophy —— or, if that could be hoped, to adore the great Creator in thefe his fublimer works — if, in their paffage through it, they could be content with fuch fare as the country produces; or at leaft reconcile themfelves to it by manly exercife, and fatigue (for there is a time, when the ftomach, and the plaineft food will be found in perfect harmony) — if they could thus, inftead of corrupting the manners of an innocent people, learn to amend their own, by feeing in how narrow a compafs the wants of human life may be compreffed — a journey through thefe wild fcenes might be attended perhaps with more improvement, than a journey to Rome, or Paris. Where manners are polifhed into vicious refinement, fimplifying is the beft mode of improving; and the example of innocence is a more inftructive leffon, than any that can be taught by artifts, and literati.

But thefe parts are too often the refort of gay company, who are under no impreffions of this kind — who have no ideas, but of extending the fphere of their amufements — or, of varying a life of diffipation. The grandeur of the country is not taken into the queftion: or, at leaft it is no otherwife confidered, than as affording fome new mode of pleafurable enjoyment. Thus even the diverfions of Newmarket are introduced — diverfions, one would imagine, more foreign to the nature of this country, than any other. A number of horfes are carried into the middle of a lake in a flat boat. A plug is drawn from the bottom: the boat finks, and the horfes are left floating on the furface. In different

ferent directions they make to land; and the horse, which arrives soonest, secures the prize.

Strenua nos exercet inertia · navibus atque
Quadrigis petimus bene vivere. Quod petis, hic est:
Est Ulubris, animus si te non deficit æquus.

SECT. XIX.

HAVING spent two hours at Patterdale, in refreshing our horses, and in surveying the beauty of it's situation; we left it with regret, and set out for Penrith.

We had now the whole length of the lake to skirt; part of which we had already traversed in our rout from Gobray-park: but we felt no reluctance at taking a second view of it.

As we traversed the two woody promontories, which we had passed in the morning, we had a grand exhibition of the middle reach of the lake; which, I have observed, is by far the longest. Martindale-fell, shooting into the water, which before adorned the left of the landscape, now took it's station on the right. The left was composed of the high woody grounds about Gobray-park.—In the center, the hills gently declining, formed a boundary at the bottom of the lake; stretching far to the east.—As a foreground, we had the woods, and rocks of the two promontories, through which we passed.

Such were the outlines, and composition of the view before us; but it's colouring was still more exquisite.

The sun was now descending low, and cast the broad shades of evening athwart the landscape, while his beams, gleaming with yellow lustre through the vallies, spread over the inlightened summits of the mountains, a thousand lovely tints—in sober harmony, where some deep recess was faintly shadowed—in splendid hue, where jutting knolls, or promontories received the fuller radiance of the diverging ray. The air was still: the lake, one vast expanse of crystal mirror. The mountain-shadows, which sometimes give the water a deep, black hue (in many circumstances, extremely picturesque,) were softened

here

here into a mild, blue tint, which fwept over half the furface. The other half received the fair impreffion of every radiant form, that glowed around. The inverted landfcape was touched in fainter colours, than the real one. Yet it was more than *laid in*. It was almoft finifhed. The laft touches alone were wanting.

What an admirable ftudy for the pallet is fuch a fcene as this! infinitely beyond the camera's contracted bounds. Here you fee nature in her full dimenfions. You are let into the very myftery—into every artifice, of her pencil. In the *reflected picture*, you fee the *ground fhe lays in*—the great effects preferved—and that veil of expreffive obfcurity thrown over all, in which what is done, is done fo exquifitely, that if you wifh the *finifhing touches*, you wifh them only by the fame inimitable hand that gave the fketch. Turn from the fhadow to the reality, and you have them. There the obfcurity is detailed. The picture, and the fketch reflect mutual graces on each other.

I dwell the longer on this view of Ullefwater, becaufe during five days, which we fpent in this romantic country, where we took a

view

view of fo many lakes, this was the only moment, in which we were fo fortunate, as to fee the water in a *pure*, reflecting ftate. Partial exhibitions of the kind we had often met with: but here we were prefented with an exhibition of this kind in it's utmoft magnificence.

Having examined this very lovely landfcape, fo perfect both in compofition, and in colouring, we proceeded in our rout along the lake.

We now re-entered Gobray park; which afforded us, for near three miles, a great variety of beautiful fcenes on the left, compofed of rocky, and broken-ground, foreft-trees, copfe-wood, and wooded hills: while the lake, and mountains, whofe fummits were now glowing with the full fplendor of an evening fun, were a continued fund of varied entertainment on the right. The eye was both amufed, and relieved by furveying the two different modes of fcenery in fucceffion: the broad fhades, and bright diverfified tints, of the diftant mountains, on one fide; and the beautiful forms, and objects of the foreground, on the other.

One

One part of the foreground was marked with singular wildness. It was a kind of rocky pass near the margin of the lake; known, I believe, by the name of *Yew-cragg*. If Cæsar had seen it, it would have struck him in a military light; and he would have described it as a defile, "angustum, & difficile, inter montem, & lacum; quo vix singuli carri ducerentur. Mons altissimus impendebat; ut facile perpauci transitum prohibere possent*."

But our imaginations were more amused with picturesque, than military ideas. It struck us therefore merely as an object of beauty.—It's features were these.

At a little distance from the lake, the broken side of a mountain falls abruptly to the ground in two noble tiers of rock; both which are shattered in every direction. The rocks were ornamented in the richest manner with wood. The road skirted the lake; and between it and the rocks, all was rough, broken-ground, intangled with brakes, and impassable. Among the rocks arose a grove of forest-trees,

* Cæf. Com. Lib. 1.

of various height, according to the inequality of the ground. Here and there, a few scattered oaks, the fathers of the foreſt, reared their peeled, and withered trunks acroſs the glade, and ſet off the vivid green of the more luxuriant trees. The deer ſtarting from the brakes, as the feet of our horſes approached, added new wildneſs to the native character of the view; while the ſcreams of a hernery (the wildeſt notes in nature) allowed the ear to participate in the effect.

The illumination of this grand maſs of rock was as intereſting, as the compoſition of it It was overſpread, when we ſaw it, with a deep evening-ſhadow, with many a darker tint in the cloſer receſſes. A mild ray, juſt tinged with the bluſh of a ſetting ſun, tipped the ſummits of the trees:

>While, ruſhing through the branches, rifted cliffs
>Dart their *white* heads, and *glitter* through the *gloom.*

Were a man diſpoſed to turn hermit, I know not where he could fix his abode more agreeably than here. The projecting rocks would
afford

afford a sheltered situation for his cell; which would open to a scene every way-fitted for meditation. He might wander along the bottom of a mountain; and by the side of a lake, unfrequented, except by the foot of curiosity; or of some hasty shepherd, seeking for the stragglers of his flock. Here he might enjoy the contemplation of nature in all her simplicity and grandeur. This single landscape, the mere invirons of his cell, under all the varieties of light, and shade — sun-shine, and storm — morning, and evening, would itself afford an inexhausted fund of entertainment: while the ample tome expended daily before his eye, would banish the littleness of life; and naturally impress his mind with great ideas.

From this wild scene we soon entered another of a different cast. It was a circular plain, about half a mile in diameter; surrounded by mountains, with an opening to the lake. The plain was smooth, but varied; the mountains, rather low, but rugged.

A valley,

A valley, like this, confidered as a *whole*, has little picturefque beauty. But a picturefque eye will find it's objects even here. It will inveftigate the hills, and pick out fuch portions, as are moft pleafing. Thefe it will form into backgrounds, and inrich the foreground (which can only be a plain) with cattle, trees, or other objects.— Even fuch fimple fcenes, by the aid of judicious lights, may form pictures.

We had the fame kind of view foon after, repeated — a circular valley, furrounded with mountains, tho varied in many particulars from the other. Both however were equally unadorned; and as both were capable, by a few well-chofen accompaniments, of being formed into good pictures; fo likewife both were capable of being made delightful fcenes in nature, by a little judicious planting; tho we muft ftill have wifhed this planting to have had the growth of a century.

It is remarkable, that we find scarce any disposition of ground, that belongs to a mountainous country, of which Virgil has not taken notice. The scenes we now examined, he exactly describes: only he has given his hills the ornament of wood, which he knew was their most picturesque dress.

——————————————— Tendit
Gramineum in campum, quem collibus undique curvis
Cingebant sylvæ, mediaque in valle theatri
Circus erat. ————————————

Not far from these circular plains stands *Gobray-hall*; once the capital of these domains; but now a neglected mansion. If situation can recommend a place, this seems to enjoy one in great perfection. It stands on high ground, with higher still behind it. We did not ride up to the house; but it seemed to command a noble view of the lake, and of the scenery around it.

Nearly at the point where Ullefwater makes it's last curve, stands the village of *Water-Mullock*;

Mullock; situated rather within the land. Through this place the road carried us to the last reach of the lake; which is the least beautiful part. Here the hills grow smooth, and lumpish; and the country, at every step, loses some of the wild strokes of nature; and degenerates, if I may so speak, into cultivation.

At the end of the lake stands *Dunmallet*, a remarkable hill, which overlooks the last reach; but is itself rather a disgusting object. Shaped with conic exactness; planted uniformly with Scotch firs; and cut as uniformly into walks verging to a center, it becomes a vile termination of a noble view.——— Once probably it was more interesting; when the Roman eagle was planted, as it formerly was, upon it's summit — when it's bold, rough sides were in unison with the objects around — and a noble castle frowned, from it's precipices over the lake. This fortress, whose ramparts may yet be traced, must once have been of considerable importance, as it commanded all the avenues of the country.

We

We had now finished our view of Ullef-water, which contains a wonderful variety of grand, and picturesque scenes, compressed within a very narrow compass.—In one part, not far from Water-Mullock, the road carried us to the higher grounds, from whence we had a view of the whole lake, and all it's vast accompaniments together—a troubled sea of mountains; a broken scene—amusing, but not picturesque.

In our evening-ride, we had skirted only one side of the lake; and wished our time would have allowed us to skirt the other also. It is probable the southern coast might have afforded very noble distant views of the woods, and rocks of Gobray-park, and the adjacent lofty grounds.

We could have wished also to have navigated the lake: for though views from the *water*, are in general less beautiful, than the same views from the *land*, as they want the advantage of a foreground, and alfo bring the horizon too low*; yet it is probable the grand reaches of this lake, and the woody promontories, round which the water winds, would have difplayed many beautiful paffages from a boat.

One view from the water, we heard much commended, that of the laft reach of the lake, towards the conic hill of Dunmallet. The fides of the lake — it's gliding away into the river Eamot, which carries it off — Poolybridge, which is thrown over that river, at the bottom of the lake — and the country beyond — were all much extolled: but we could not conceive, that any views, at this end of the lake, could be comparable to what we had feen near the fhores of Patterdale: efpecially any views, in which the regular form of Dunmallet made fo confiderable a part.

It would have added alfo to our amufement, to have taken a view of the lake by moonlight.

---

* See page 96. Vol. 1.

light. For tho it is very difficult *in painting* to manage so feeble an effusion of light in such a manner, as, at the same time, to *illumine objects*, and *produce an effect*; yet the reality, in such scenes as these, is attended often with a wonderful solemnity and grandeur. That shadowy form of great objects, which is sometimes traced out by a silver thread, and sometimes by a kind of bright obscurity on a darker ground, almost oppresses the imagination with sublime ideas. Effects also we sometimes see of light and shade, tho only faintly marked. In the absence of colour, the clair-obscure is more striking;

> —————— one expanded sheet of light
> Diffusing. while the shades (from rock to rock
> Irregularly thrown,) with solemn gloom
> Diversify the whole. ——————

I cannot leave the scenes of Ullesvvater, without taking notice of an uncommon fish, which frequents it's waters; and which is equally the object of the naturalist, and of the epicure. It is of the trout-species; beautifully clad in scales of silver; firm, and finely flavoured;

flavoured; and of such dimensions, that it has sometimes been known to weigh between thirty and forty pounds. The same species is found in the lake of Geneva; and, I believe, in other lakes.

Having now past the limits of the lake, we traversed a very pleasant country in our road to Penrith, keeping the Eamot commonly within view on our right; and leaving on the left, the ruins of Dacre-castle, the ancient seat of the noble family of that name.

No part of Cumberland is more inhabited by the genteeler families of the county than this. Within the circumference of a few miles stand many of their houses; some of which have formerly been castles: but the road carried us in view only of two or three of them.

Before we arrived at Penrith, one of these fortresses, which is known by the name of Penrith-castle, presented us with a very noble ruin, and under the most interesting circumstances.

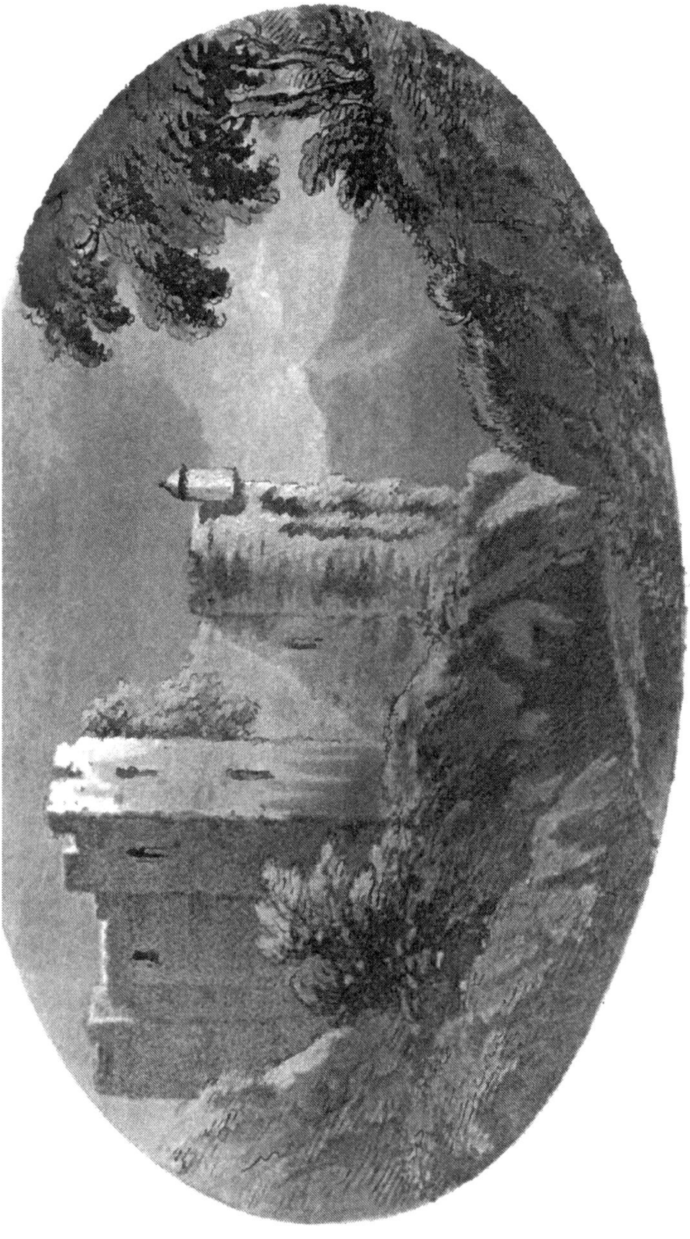

ſtances. The ſun, which, through the length of a ſummer-day, had befriended us with all his morning, noon, and evening powers, preparing now, with *farewel ſweet*, to take his leave, gave us yet one more beautiful exhibition.

A grand broken arch preſented itſelf firſt in deep ſhadow. Through the aperture appeared a part of the internal ſtructure, thrown into perſpective to great advantage; and illumined by the departing ray. Other fragments of the ſhattered towers, and battlements were juſt touched with the ſplendid tint: but the body of light reſted on thoſe parts, which were ſeen through the ſhadowed arch.

In the offskip, beyond the caſtle, aroſe a hill, in ſhadow likewiſe; on the top of which ſtood a lonely beacon. The windows anſwering each other, we could juſt diſcern the glowing horizon through them — a circumſtance, which however trivial in deſcription, has a beautiful effect in landſcape. — This beacon is a monument of thoſe tumultuous times, which preceded the union; and the only monument of the kind now remaining in theſe parts; though ſuch beacons were formerly ſtationed over the whole country;

and could spread intelligence, in a few seconds from one end of it to the other.

At this later day these castles and posts of alarm, adorning the country, they once defended, raise pleasing reflections on a comparison of present times with past — those turbulent times, when no man could sleep in safety unless secured by a fortress. In war he feared the invasion of an open enemy: and in peace a mischief still more formidable, the ravages of banditti; with whom the country was always at that time infested. These wretches were composed of the outlaws from both nations; and inhabiting the fastnesses of bogs, and mountains, used to sally out, and plunder in all directions.

Penrith is a neat town, situated not unpleasantly, under mountains; and in the neighbourhood of lakes.

In the church-yard we saw an ancient monument, which has occasioned much speculation among antiquarians. It consists of two rough pillars, with four semicircular stones, fixed in the ground between them. Dr. Todd, an antiquarian of the last age, found out four
wild-

wild-boars, and other ingenious devices, on the different parts of this monument. We examined it with attention: but could not find even the moſt diſtant reſemblance of any form in nature. The whole ſurface ſeemed to be nothing more than a piece of rough chiſſel-work.——— In the church, which is a handſome, plain ſtructure, is placed a ſtone, recording the ravages of the plague among the ſeveral towns of this neighbourhood, in the year 1598.

As we leave Penrith, which is within twenty miles of Carliſle, we enter that vaſt waſte, called *Inglewood-foreſt*, through which we rode at leaſt nine miles; in all which ſpace there is ſcarce a tree to be ſeen; and yet were it well planted, as it once probably was, many parts of it might be admired: for the ground makes bold and noble ſwells; the back ſcenery is compoſed of a grand ſweep of mountains; and on the left, are diſtant views into a cultivated country.

The mountains, which adorn theſe ſcenes, are the ſame we ſaw, as we left Keſwick; only the more northern part of that circular chain is now turned towards us. In this view, the ridge of Saddle-back assumes that shape, from which it derives it's appellation.

That part of Inglewood-forest, which lies nearest the town, is known by the name of Penrith-fell, consisting of rough, and hilly grounds. One of the highest hills is occupied by the beacon, of which we had a distant view, as we examined the ruins of Penrith-castle.

On this spot, in the year 1715, the Cumberland militia assembled to oppose the rebels in their march to the south. But a militia without discipline, is never formidable. The whole body fled, as the van of the rebels appeared marching round an opposite hill.

Nicolson, bishop of Carlisle, a strenuous man, who had been very instrumental in bringing them together, and now attended their march; was so chagrined, and mortified at their behaviour, that in a fit of obstinate vexation, he would not quit the field. The enemy was coming on apace. His servants rode up to the coach for orders. The bishop sat mute with indignation. All thoughts of
himself

himself were lost in the public disgrace. His coachman however, whose feelings were less delicate, thinking the management of affairs, in this interruption of government, now devolved upon him, lashed his horses, and carried his master off the field.

On the verge of the forest, at a place called Plumpton, a large Roman station (or stative camp) runs a quarter of a mile, on the right. You trace the ground broken variously, where tents, kitchens, and earthern tables probably stood, not unlike the vestiges of a modern encampment. On the left appear the lines of a fort of considerable dimensions, about one hundred and fifty yards square, which was once the citadel of this military colony. The ramparts, and ditches may easily be traced on every side.

The great road indeed, which we travelled, is intirely Roman; and is laid almost by a line over the forest. You seldom see a *winding* road of Roman construction. Their surveyors, and pioneers had no idea of the line of beauty; nor stood in reverence of any inclosures; but always took the shortest cut; making the

Appian

Appian way the model of all their provincial roads.

At Ragmire, about a mile farther, where the road croffes a bog, large wooden frame-works, yet uninjured by time, were lately dug up; which the Romans had laid, as a foundation for their caufey, over that un-ftable furface.

On leaving Inglewood-foreft, the road enters an inclofed country, in which is little variety, and fcarce an interefting object, till we arrive at Carlifle.

The approach to that city, from the rifing ground, near the little village of Hereby is grand. The town, which terminates a vifta of a mile in length, takes a very compact form; in which no part is feen, but what makes a handfome appearance. The fquare, and maffy tower of the caftle rifes on the right: in the middle, the cathedral rifes ftill higher; and contiguous to it, on the left, appear the round towers of the citadel; which was built by Henry VIII. in the form of all
his

his caftles on the Hampfhire, and Kentifh coafts.

The beauty however of this approach is foon loft. As we defcend the hill from Hereby, the town finks into the infignificance of it's invirons.

The entrance is ftill beautiful; the road winding to the gate round the towers of the citadel.

SECT. XX.

FEW towns offer a fairer field to an antiquary, than Carlifle. It's origin, and hiftory, are remote, curious and obfcure. It was unqueftionably a place of confequence in Roman times. Severus's wall juft includes it in the Britifh pale. The veftiges of that barrier run within half a mile of it's gates, and it probably figured firft under the character of a fortrefs, on that celebrated rampart.

In after ages it had it's fhare fucceffively in the hiftory of Saxons, Danes, and Scots; and during the revolutions of thefe feveral nations, was the fcene of every viciffitude of war. It hath been frequently befieged, pillaged, burnt and rebuilt. Once it lay buried in it's ruins for the fpace of two centuries. Rufus brought it again into exiftence. The prefent town is founded on the veftiges of
former

former towns; which in many parts have raifed the ground within, nearly to the height of the walls. The foundations of a houfe are rarely dug without difturbing the ruins of fome other houfe. It has been the refidence; and it has been the prifon of kings. An old afh-tree is ftill fhewn, near the gate of the caftle; which is faid to have been planted by the unfortunate Mary of Scotland, who fpent a part of her captivity in this fortrefs; whither fhe was foon brought, after her landing at Workington. Many princes alfo have fhed their royal favours on this ancient town; and made it's fortifications their care.

Now all it's military honours are difgraced. Northern commotions are no longer dreaded. It's gates ftand always open; and it's walls, the object of no farther attention, are falling faft into ruin. The firing of a morning and an evening gun from the caftle, which was the laft garrifon-form that remained, hath been difcontinued thefe fix years, to the great regret of the country around, whofe hours of labour it regulated.

But

But I mean not to enter into the hiftory of Carlifle: it concerns me only as an object of beauty. Within it's walls indeed it contains little that deferves notice. The caftle is heavy in all it's parts, as thefe fabrics commonly are. It is too perfect to afford much pleafure to the picturefque eye; except as a remote object, foftened by diftance. Hereafter, when it's fhattered towers, and buttreffes, give a lightnefs to it's parts, it may adorn fome future landfcape.

The cathedral deferves ftill lefs attention. It is a heavy, Saxon pile; and there is nothing about it, that is beautiful; except the eaftwindow, which is a rich, and very elegant piece of Gothic ramification.

The *fratry*, as it is called, or chapter-houfe, in the abbey, is the only building that deferves notice. On one fide, where it has formerly been connected with the cloyfters, it has little beauty: but on the other, next the deanery, it's proportions and ornaments are elegant. It feems to be of that ftyle of architecture, which prevailed rather before the two later Henries.

But

But though Carlisle furnishes little amusement within it's walls; yet it adds great beauty, as a distant object, to the country around. Few towns enjoy a better situation. It stands on a rising ground, in the midst of meadows, watered by two considerable rivers; which flowing on different sides of the city, unite a little below it; and form the whole ground-plot, on which it stands, into a kind of peninsula. Beyond the meadows, the ground rises, in almost all parts, at different distances.

The meadows around it, especially along the banks of the river Eden, want only a little more wood to make them very beautiful. In high floods, which happen two or three times in the course of a winter, they exhibit a very grand scene. The town appears standing out, like a promontory in the midst of a vast lake.

The short siege which Carlisle sustained in the rebellion, of the year 1745, together with some awkward circumstances that attended it, threw
a general

a general odium upon the town; and many believed, among whom was the late duke of Cumberland, that it was very ill-affected to the government. No suspicion was ever more unjust. I dare take upon me to say, there were scarce half a dozen people in the whole place, who wished well to the rebellion.

The following anecdote, known but to few; and totally unknown till many years after the event, will throw some light on it's hasty surrender; which brought disgrace on it's political principles.

When the rebels came before it, it was garrisoned only by two companies of invalids; and two raw, undisciplined regiments of militia. General Wade lay at Newcastle with a considerable force: and the governor of Carlisle informing him, how unprovided he was, begged a reinforcement. The single hope of this relief, enabled the gentlemen of the country, who commanded the militia, to keep their men under arms.

In the mean time the rebels were known to be as ill-prepared for an attack, as the town was for a defence. They had now lain a week before it; and found it was impracticable, for want of artillery, to make any attempt. They feared alſo an interruption from general Wade: and beſides, were unwilling to delay any longer their march towards London. Under theſe difficulties, they had come to a reſolution to abandon their deſign.

At this critical juncture the governor of Carliſle received a letter from general Wade, informing him, he was ſo circumſtanced, that he could not poſſibly ſend the reinforcement that had been deſired. This mortifying intelligence, tho not publickly known, was however communicated to the principal officers; and to ſome others: among whom was a buſy attorney, whoſe name was H———s.

H———s was then addreſſing a young lady, the daughter of Mr. F———r, a gentleman of the country, and to aſſiſt his cauſe, and give himſelf conſequence with his intended father in law, he whiſpered to him, among his other political ſecrets, the diſappointment from general Wade.

The whiſper did not reſt here. F———r frequented a club in the neighbourhood; where obſerving (in the jollity of a chearful evening) that only friends were preſent, he gave his company the information he had juſt received from H———s.

There

There was in that company, one S——d, a gentleman of some fortune near Carlisle, who, tho a known papist, was however at that time, thought to be of very intire affection to the government. This man, possessed of such a secret, and wishing for an opportunity to serve a cause, which he favoured in his heart, took horse that very night, after he left the club-room, and rode directly to the rebel-camp; which he found under orders to break up the next morning. He was carried immediately to the duke of Perth, and others of the rebel leaders, to whom he communicated his intelligence; and assured them, they might expect a mutiny in the town, if they continued before it, one day longer. Counter orders were immediately issued; and the next day the Cumberland and Westmoreland militia began to mutiny and disperse: and the town defended now only by two companies of invalids, was thought no longer tenable. The governor was tried by a court-martial; and acquitted: and nobody supposed that either the militia-officers, or their men, were impressed by any motive worse than fear.

In ſo variegated a country, as England, there are few parts, which do not afford many pleaſing, and picturefque views. The moſt probable way of finding them, as I obſerved a little above, is to follow the courſe of the rivers. About their banks we ſhall uſually find the richeſt ſcenery, which the country can produce. This rule we followed in the few excurſions, which we had time to make from Carliſle: and firſt we took a view of the river Cauda.

Near the town this river is broken into ſo many ſtreams; and throws up, every where, ſo many barren beds of pebbles, that there is no great beauty in this part of it's courſe. But above, where higher banks confine it's impetuoſity, it becomes more intereſting. The vales of Sebergham and Dalſton, we heard much commended. The former we did not viſit: the latter we followed, many miles, along it's winding couiſe; and found ourſelves often in the midſt of beautiful ſcenes; the river being ſhut up ſometimes by cloſe and lofty banks,

and

and sometimes flowing through meadows edged with wood.

Among other situations on the Cauda we were much pleased with that of Rose-castle, the seat of the bishop of Carlisle: which stands on a gentle rise, in a wide part of the vale; the river winding round it, in a semi-circular form, at about half a mile's distance. The ground between the castle, and the river, consists of beautiful meadows; and beyond the river, a lofty bank, winding with it, and well planted, forms a sweep of hanging wood. The castle composed of square towers, tho no object on the spot, is a good ornament to the scene.

Between Rose-castle and Wigton the country abounds with the relicks of Roman incampments. At a place, called Chalk-cliff (which, by the way, is a cliff of red stone) this legionary inscription is engraven in the native rock.

$$\text{LEG } \overline{\overline{\text{II}}} \text{ AVG}$$
$$\text{MILITES FEC.}$$
$$\text{COH } \overline{\text{III}} \text{ COH } \overline{\text{IIII}}$$

From the Cauda, our next excursion was along the Eden. On the banks of this river, we were informed of many interesting scenes. At Kirkofwal, and Nunnery particularly, the country was represented as very engaging; but Corby-castle, about five miles from Carlisle, was the only place above the town, which we had time to visit.

At Wetherall we ferried over the river; and landed under the castle, which stands on the edge of a lofty bank. This bank stretches at least three miles along the course of the river, partly below, but chiefly above the castle. I give it it's ancient title; tho it is now a mere modern house, without the least vestige of it's former dignity. Below the castle, the bank is rocky, and falls precipitately into the water; above, it makes a more gentle descent; and leaves an edging, which, in some parts, spreads into little winding meads, and where it is narrowest, is broad enough for a handsome walk. The whole bank, both above, and below the castle, is covered with wood, large oak, and ash; and in many places the scenery is rocky also. But the rocks are not of the grey kind,

stained

ftained with a variety of different tints — the *saxa circumlita mufco:* but incline rather to a fandy red, which is not the moft coalefcing hue. They give however great fpirit, and beauty to the fcene.

The bank of the river, *oppofite* to the caftle, is likewife high; in many parts woody; in others affording an intermixture of wood, and lawn. Here ftand the ruins of Wetherall-abbey; tho little more of it is left, than a fquare tower, which is fome ornament, tho no very picturefque one, to the fcene. Thefe ruins were once extenfive, and, I have heard, beautiful; but the dean and chapter of Carlifle, to whom the place belongs, fome years ago carried off the ftones, with more œconomy than tafte, to build a prebendal houfe.

On this fide of the river alfo, an object prefents itfelf, known by the name of *Wetherall-fafeguard*, which is efteemed a great curiofity. It confifts of three chambers cut in the folid rock, which being in this part almoft a precipice, the accefs to the chambers is difficult. It is fuppofed to have been an appendage of the abbey; where the monks, in times of diforder, fecreted their wealth. Some antiquarians fuppofe it to have been inhabited by a

religious

religious devotee, and call it *St. Conftantine's cell.* It is rather a curious place, than any great ornament to the fcene.

To all thefe natural advantages of the fcenery about Corby-caftle, the improvements of art have added little. The late proprietor, who had feen nothing himfelf; and imagined from the refort of ftrangers to fee the beauty of his fituation, that they admired his tafte, refolved to make Corby one of the moft fumptuous places in Europe. With this view, he fcooped his rocks into grottos — fabricated a cafcade, confifting of a lofty flight of regular ftone fteps — cut a ftraight walk through his woods, along the banks of the river; at the end of which he reared a temple: and being refolved to add every ornament, that expence could procure, he hired an artift of the country, at four-pence a day (for labour was then cheap) to make ftatues. Numberlefs were the works of this genius. Diana, Neptune, Polyphemus, Nymphs and Satyrs in abundance, and a variety of other figures, became foon the ornaments of the woods; and met the eye of the fpectator wherever he turned. A punfter, who was remarkable for making only one good pun in his life, made it here. Pointing to one of thefe
ftrange

ftrange figures, he called it *a fatyr upon the place*.

But the tafte of the prefent age hath deftroyed the pride of the laft. The prefent proprietor hath done little; but what he hath done, is done well. The rocks indeed fcooped into holes, can never be reftored to their native fimplicity, and grandeur. Their bold projections are for ever effaced. Nor could a century reftore thofe trees, which were rooted up to form the vifta. But the ftatues, like the ancient fculpture of the Egyptians, are now no more. The temple is going faft into ruin: and the cafcade (fo frivolous, if it had even been good in it's kind, on the banks of a great, and rapid river) is now overgrown with thickets. The old line of the walk could not eafily be effaced. but a new one, beyond the temple, is carried on, which follows naturally the courfe of the river. And indeed this part of the walk admits more beauty, than any other; for the varieties of ground are greater; the bank, and edging of meadow, are more irregular; and the river more finuous.

This walk having conducted us along the river, through thefe pleafing irregularities, about two miles from the caftle, climbs the higher grounds, and returns through woods, and beautiful fheep walks, which lie on the fides, and fummit of the bank. Through the whole of it, both at the top, and bottom, are many pleafant views; but they are all of the more confined kind.

Many parts of this walk were wrought by the prieft of the family, which is a popifh branch of the Howards. He belongs to an order, which enjoins it's members to manual labour fo many hours in the day; laying them, with admirable wifdom, under the *wholefome neceffity* of acquiring health, and fpirits. I am perfuaded that if a ftudious man were *obliged* to dig three or four hours a day, he would ftudy the better, during the remaining part of it. We had been recommended to the civilities of this ecclefiaftic (the family being then in France,) and found him at work in the garden. He received us politely; and difcovered the manners of a gentleman, under the garb of a day-labourer, without the leaft apology for his drefs, and occupation. There is fomething very pleafing in the fimplicity and manlinefs of not being afhamed of the neceffary functions of any ftate, which we have made our option in life.— This

eccle-

ecclefiaftic fucceeded Father Walfh, who has lately engaged the attention of the public. ——
I have dwelt the longer on this fcene, as it is the moft admired one in Cumberland.

From Corby-caftle to Warwick, which lies about two miles nearer Carlifle, on the banks of the fame river, the road is beautiful. Many admire the fituation of Warwick alfo. It feems to be a fweet, retired fcene, but we had not time to view it.

The antiquarian's eye is immediately caught here by the parifh-church; the chancel of which, forming the fegment of a circle, and being pierced with fmall lancet-windows, fhews at once, that it is of Norman origin. Tho every other mark were obliterated, he will tell you, that this is evidence fufficient of it's antiquity.

SECT. XXI.

HAVING seen as much of the river Eden, above Carlisle, as our time would allow, we made our next excursion towards it's mouth, where Brugh-marsh attracted our attention. In our way we had many pleasing river views.

Brugh-marsh lies at the extremity of the English border; running up as far as Solway-frith, which, in this part, divides England from Scotland. It is a vast extended plain, flat as the surface of a quiet ocean. I do not remember that land, ever gave me before so vast an idea of space. The idea of this kind, which such scenes as Salisbury-Plain suggests, is much less pure. The inequality of the ground there, sets bounds to the idea. It is the ocean in a ftorm; in which the idea of extenfion is greatly broken, and intercepted by the turbulence of the waves. Brugh-marfh gives us the idea of folid water, rather than of land, if we except only the colour:

———————— Intermineable meads,
And vaft favannahs, where the wandering eye
Unfixt, is in a verdant ocean loft.

Brugh-marfh is one of thofe extended plains, (only more extenfive, than fuch plains commonly are) from which the fea, in a courfe of ages, hath retired. It is difficult to compute it's limits. It ranges many leagues, in every direction, from a centre (for fpace fo diffufe affumes of courfe a circular appearance) without a hedge, or even a bufh, to intercept it's bounds; till it foften into the azure mountains of the horizon. Nothing indeed, but mountains, can circumfcribe fuch a fcene. All inferior boundaries of wood, and rifing grounds are loft. On the Englifh fide it is bounded by that circular chain, in the heart of Cumberland, in which Skiddaw is preeminent. Nothing intermediate appears. On the Scotch fide it's courfe is interrupted, through the fpace of a few leagues, by Solway-frith;

frith; which spreads, when the tide is at ebb, into a vast stretch of sand. The plain however is still preserved. Having passed this sandy obstruction, it changes it's hue again into vivid green, and stretches far and wide into the Scotch border, till it's progress at length is stopped by the mountains of Galloway, and Niddsdale This extension is as much as the eye can well comprehend. Had the plain been boundless, like an Arabian desert, I know not whether it would not have lost that idea of space, which so vast a circumscription gives it.

The whole area of Brugh-marsh, (which from it's *denomination* we should suppose to be swampy,) is every where perfectly firm; and the turf, soft, bright, and pure. Scarce a weed rears it's head. Nothing appears of statelier growth than a mushroom, which spreads here in luxuriant knots.

This vast plain is far from being a desert waste. Innumerable herds of cattle pasture at large in it's rich verdure; and range, as in a state of nature.

But

But tho the primary idea, which this scene represents, arises purely from space, and is therefore an idea rather grand than picturesque; yet it is not totally incapable of picturesque embellishment. It is true, it wants almost every ingredient of landscape; on the foreground, it wants objects to preserve the keeping; and in the offskip, that profusion of little parts, which in a scene of cultivation gives richness to distance. In treating therefore a subject of this kind on canvas, recourse must be had to adventitious objects. Cattle come most naturally to hand; which being stationed, in various groups, at different distances, may serve both as a foreground to the landscape, and as a gage to the perspective.

Brugh-marsh is farther remarkable for having been the scene of one of the greatest catastrophes of the English history — the death of Edward the First. Here, after Scotland had made a third attempt to recover it's liberty, that prince, drew together the most puissant army, which England had ever seen. The Scots from their borders, saw the plain whitened with tents: but they knew not how

nearly

nearly their deliverance approached. The greatest events generally arrive unlooked for. They saw a delay; and afterwards a confusion in the mighty host before them: but they heard not, till three days after, that the soul and spirit of the enterprize was gone; and that their great adversary lay breathless in his camp.

Edward had been taken ill at Carlisle; where he had met his parliament. But neither disease, nor age (for he was now near seventy) could repress his ardour. Tho he could not mount his horse, he ordered himself to be carried in a litter to the camp; where his troops received him with acclamations of joy. But it was short-lived. The motion had irritated his disorder into a violent dysentery; which immediately carried him off.

The English borderers long revered the memory of a prince, who had so often chastised an enemy they hated: and in gratitude reared a pillar to his name; which still testifies the spot, on which he died. It stands rather on the edge of the marsh, and bears this simple inscription.

MEMORIÆ ÆTERNÆ
EDVARDI,
REGIS ANGLIÆ LONGE CLARISSIMI,
QUI, IN BELLI APPARATU
CONTRA SCOTOS OCCUPATUS,
HIC IN CASTRIS OBIIT,
7 JULII A. D. 1307.

Among other places in the neighbourhood of Carlisle, we made an excurfion into Gillsland, with an intention chiefly to fee Naworth-caftle, the vale and ruins of the Abbey of Lanercoft; and the ruins of Scaleby-caftle.

As we leave Carlisle, along the great military road to Newcaftle, the view of the river Eden from Stanwix-bank, is very pleafing. The curve it defcribes; the beautiful meadows it winds through; and the mountains, which clofe the fcene, make all together an amufing combination of objects. Wood only is wanting.

On crossing the river Irthing, about seven miles from Carlisle, the country, which was before unpleasing, becomes rich, and interesting. Here we enter the barony of Gillsland, an extensive district, which consists, in this part, of a great variety of hill, and dale. The hills are sandy, bleak, and unpleasant: but the vallies, which are commonly of the contracted kind, are beautiful. They are generally woody, and each of them watered by some little busy stream. — From these vallies, or *gills*, (as the country-people call them,) with which the whole barony abounds, Camden supposes it might possibly have taken the name of Gillsland.

On a delightful knoll, gently gliding into a sinuous *gill*, surrounded with full-grown oak, and overlooking the vale of Lanercost, stands Naworth-castle. The house, which consists of two large square towers, united by a main body, is too regular to be beautiful, unless thrown into perspective. It was formerly one of those fortified places, in which the nobility and gentry of the borders were obliged to live, in thofe times of confufion, which preceded the union. And indeed the whole internal contrivance of this caftle appears calculated either to keep an enemy out; or to elude his fearch, if he fhould happen to get in. The idea of a comfortable dwelling is totally excluded. The staterooms are few, and ordinary: but the little apartments, and hiding-holes, acceffible only by dark paffages, and blind ftair-cafes, are innumerable. Many of the clofe receffes, which it contains, are probably at this time, unknown. Nothing indeed can mark in ftronger colours the fears, and jealoufies, and caution of thofe times, than the internal ftructure of one of thefe caftles.

Naworth-caftle was formerly the capital manfion of the barons of Gillfland; who, at fo great a diftance from court, and feated in a country, at that time, untamed by law, are faid to have exercifed very extraordinary powers. The Lord William Howard, who is remembered by the name of *bald Willy*, is ftill the object of invective for his acts of tyranny. His prifons are fhewn; and the fite of his gibbets; where, in the phrafe of
the

the country, he would *head, and hang without judge or jury.* — But it is probable, that his memory is injured. He acted under a standing commission of oyer and terminer, from Elizabeth; and was one of those bold spirits, which are necessary to repress the violence of lawless times. Many acts of power undoubtedly he committed: but his difficult situation compelled him. This part of the kingdom was most harrassed by those troops of mischievous banditti; whom I have just had occasion to mention. They were a numerous, and not an ill-regulated body, acting under leaders, whom a spirit of enterprize raised to power. These miscreants, in times even of profoundest peace, kept in constant exercise the wariness and activity of the chiefs of the country. Sometimes they would plunder in large bodies; and sometimes in little pilfering bands. When they were taken in the fact; or, as it was called, by the *bloody hand*, they were put to instant death. In other cases a jury was impannelled.

The active chief, who gave occasion to this digression, seems to have lived in as much terror himself, as he spread among others. He had contrived a sort of citadel in his own castle;

castle; a room, which is still shewn, with an iron door, where he constantly slept, and where his armour lies rusting to this day. From him the earls of Carlisle are descended; and have been, in succession, the proprietors of Naworth-castle.

As we left this old fortress, and descended the hill towards the ruins of the abbey of Lanercost, which lie about two miles farther, the whole vale, in which they are seated, opened before us. It is esteemed one of the most pleasing scenes in the country; and indeed we found it such. It's area is about half a mile in breadth, and two or three miles in length, consisting of one ample sweep. The sides, which are gentle declivities, are covered thick with wood, in which larger depredations have been lately made, than are consistent with picturesque beauty. — At the distant end of the vale, where the woods appear to unite, the river Irthing enters; which is considerable enough, tho divided into two channels, to be fully adequate to the scene.— The banks of the river, and indeed the whole area of the vale, are sprinkled with clumps, and

and single trees; which have a good effect in breaking the lines, and regular continuity of the side-skreens; and in hiding, here and there, the course of the river; especially the bridges, which would otherwise be too bare and formal.

Near that extremity of the vale, which is opposite to Naworth-castle, lies the abbey. At a distance it forms a good object, rising among the woods. As you approach, it begins to raise a disappointment: and on the spot, it is but an unpleasing ruin. The whole is a heavy, Saxon pile; compressed together without any of that airy lightness, which accompanies the Gothic. Scarce one *detached* fragment appears in any point of view. The tower is low, and without either form, or ornament; and one of the great ailes is modernized into an awkward parish-church. The only beautiful part of the whole is the east end. It is composed of four broken ailes; every wall of which consists of two tiers of arches, affording a very unusual appearance; and at the same time a very amusing confusion, from the uncommon multiplication of so many arches, and pillars. —— This part of the abbey seems to have been a separate chapel;

chapel; or perhaps an oratory belonging to the noble family of Dacre, which had once poffeffions in thefe parts. Here lie the remains of feveral ancient chiefs of that houfe; whofe fepulchral honours are now almoft intirely obliterated. Their blazoned arms, and Gothic tombs, many of which are fumptuous, are fo matted with briars, and thiftles, that even the foot of curiofity is kept at a diftance.

Except thefe remains of the abbey-church no other parts of this ancient monaftery are now left; but an old gateway; and a fquare building, patched into a farm-houfe, which has no beauty.

In returning to Carlifle we paffed through the valley of Cambeck, which contains fome pleafing fcenery; and a very confiderable Roman ftation, on a high bank at *Caftle-fteeds*.

Rivers often prefent us with very moral analogies; their characters greatly refembling thofe of men. The violent, the reftlefs, the fretful, the active, the fluggifh, the gentle, the bounteous, and many other epithets, belong equally to both. The little ftream, which

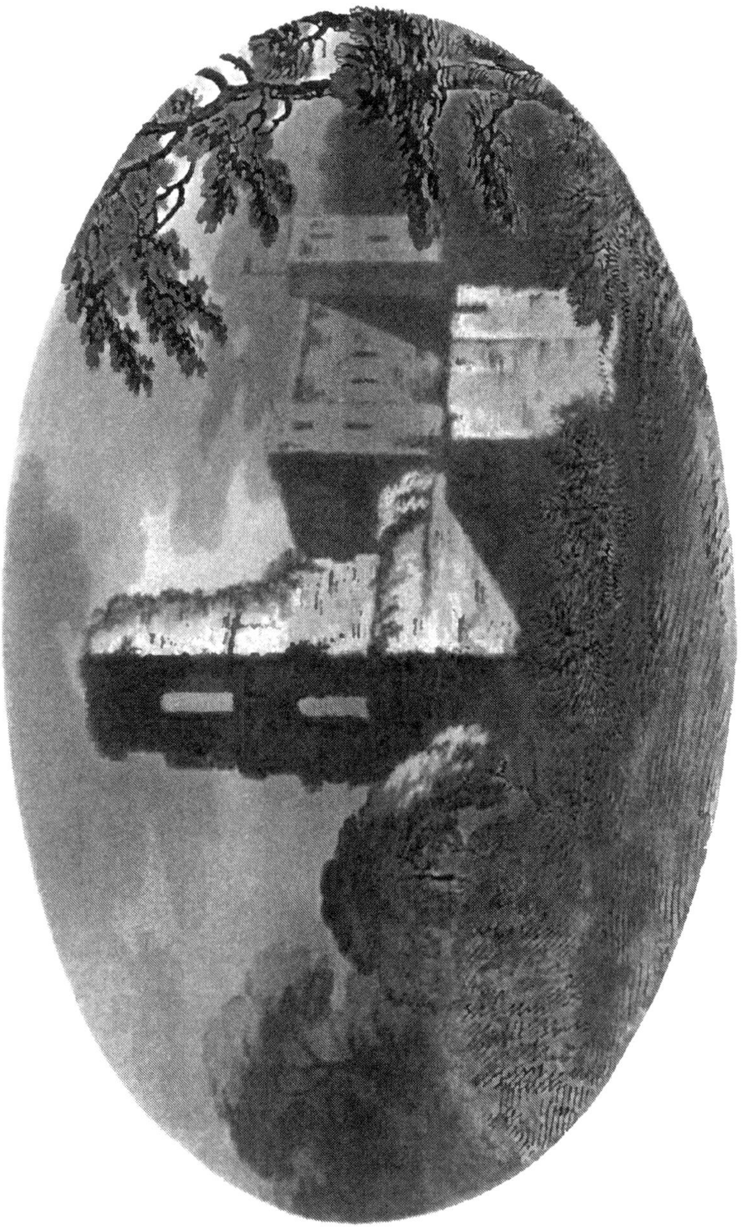

which divides the valley of Cambeck, suggested the analogy. It's whole courfe is marked with acts of violence. In every part you fee heaps of barren fand, and gravel, which in it's furious moods it has thrown up, fometimes on one fide, and fometimes on another; deftroying every where the little fcenes of beauty, and plots of cultivation.

About three miles farther we vifited the ruins of Scaleby-caftle. This was another of thofe fortified houfes, which are fo frequent in this country.

It ftands, as caftles rarely do, on a flat; and yet, tho it's fite be ill adapted to any modes of defence, it has been a place of more than ordinary ftrength. Rocks, knolls, and bold, projecting promontories, on which caftles ufually ftand, fuggeft various advantages of fituation; and generally determine the kind of ftructure. On a flat, the engineer was at liberty to choofe his own. Every part was alike open to affault.

He firft drew two circular motes around the fpot he defigned to fortify: the circumference of the outward circle was fomewhat more than
half

half a mile. The earth, thrown out of thefe two motes, which were broad and deep, feems to have been heaped up at the centre, where there is a confiderable rife. On this was built the caftle, which was entered by two drawbridges; and defended by a high tower, and a very lofty wall.

At prefent, one of the motes only remains. The other is filled up; but may ftill be traced. The caftle is more perfect, than fuch buildings commonly are. The walls are very intire; and great part of the tower, which is fquare, is ftill left. It preferved it's perfect form, till the civil wars of the laft century; when the caftle, in too much confidence of it's ftrength, fhut it's gates againft Cromwell, then marching into Scotland; who made it a monument of his vengeance.

What fhare of picturefque genius Cromwell might have, I know not. Certain however it is, that no man, fince Henry the eighth, has contributed more to adorn this country with picturefque ruins. The difference between thefe two mafters lay chiefly in the ftyle of ruins, in which they compofed. Henry adorned his landfcapes with the ruins of abbeys; Cromwell, with thofe of caftles.

I have

I have seen many pieces by this master, executed in a very grand style; but seldom a finer monument of his masterly hand than this. He has rent the tower, and demolished two of it's sides, the edges of the other two he has shattered into broken lines. The chasm discovers the whole plan of the internal structure — the vestiges of the several stories — the insertion of the arches, which supported them — the windows for speculation; and the breastwork for assault.

The walls of this castle are uncommonly magnificent. They are not only of great height, but of great thickness; and defended by a large bastion; which appears to be of more modern workmanship. The greatest part of them is chambered within, and wrought into secret recesses. A massy portcullis gate leads to the ruins of what was once the habitable part of the castle, in which a large vaulted hall is the most remarkable apartment; and under it, are dark, and capacious dungeons.

The area within the mote, which consists of several acres, was originally intended to support the cattle, which should be driven thither in times of alarm. When the house was inhabited (whose chearful and better

days

days are still remembered,) this area was the garden; and all around, on the outside of the mote stood noble trees, irregularly planted, the growth of a century. Beneath the trees ran a walk round the castle; to which the situation naturally gave that pleasing curve, which in modern days hath been so much the object of art. This walk might admit of great embellishment. On one hand, it commands the ruins of the castle in every point of view; on the other, a country, which tho flat, is not unpleasing; consisting of extensive meadows, (which a little planting might turn into beautiful lawns,) bounded by lofty mountains.

This venerable pile has now undergone a second ruin. The old oaks and elms, the ancient natives of the scene, are felled. Weeds, and spiry grass have taken possession of the courts, and obliterated the very plan of a garden: while the house itself, (whose hospitable roof deserved a better fate,) is now a scene of desolation. Two wretched families, the only inhabitants of the place, occupied the two ends of the vaulted hall, when we saw it, th fragment of a tattered curtain, reaching half way to the top, being the simple boundary of their respective limits. All the rest was
waste:

waste: no other part of the house was habitable. The chambers unwindowed, and almost unroofed, fluttering with rags of ancient tapestry, were the haunt of daws, and pigeons; which burst out in clouds of dust, when the doors were opened: while the floors, yielding to the tread, made curiosity dangerous. A few pictures, heir-looms of the wall, which have long deserved oblivion, by I know not what fate, were the only appendages of this dissolving pile, which had triumphed over the injuries of time.

Shakespear's castle of Macbeth could not have been more the haunt of swallows and martins. We saw them every where about the ruins; either twittering on broken coins; threading some fractured arch; or pursuing each other, in screaming circles, round the walls of the castle *.

---

* In this old castle the author of this tour was born, and spent his early youth; which must be his apology for dwelling so long upon it. —— Since this description was written, it has, in some degree, been repaired.

SECT.

SECT. XXII.

OUR laſt expedition, in the neighbourhood of Carliſle, was to ſee the improvements of Mr. Graham of Netherby; and the ſcene or deſolation, occaſioned by the late overflowing of Solway-moſs.

Mr. Graham's improvements are not confined to a garden, or the ſpace of a mile or two around his houſe. The whole country is changed; and from a barren waſte, hath aſſumed the face — if not of beauty, at leaſt of fertility.

The domain of Netherby lies on the very ſkirts of the Engliſh border. The Romans conſidered it as a part of Caledonia; and ſhut it from the Britiſh pale. In after ages the diſtrict around it aſſumed the name of the

Debateable-land, and was the great rendezvous of thofe crews of outlawed banditti, who, under the denomination of *Mofs-troopers*, plundered the country. We have already had occafion to mention them. In this neighbourhood were the ftrong holds of many of their chiefs; particularly of Johnny Armftrong of famous memory; the noted ruins of whofe caftle are ftill extant.

Among thefe people the arts of tillage were unknown. It was abfurd to be at the trouble of fowing land themfelves, when they could fo eafily plunder the lands of others.

Tho the union of the two kingdoms put an end to the ravages on the borders; yet the manners of the inhabitants, in fome refpects, fuffered little change. Their native lazinefs, and inattention to all the arts of hufbandry, remained. They occupied large tracts of excellent land at eafy rates: but having no idea of producing yearly crops from the fame foil by culture; they ploughed their patches of ground alternately, leaving them to recover their fertility by fallows. An indolent and fcanty maintenance was all they wifhed; and this they obtained from a fmall portion of their land, with a fmall portion of their labour. Their lords in the mean time, never lived on the spot; and knew little of the state either of the country, or of it's inhabitants.

Mr. Graham immediately set himself to alter this state of things. He built a noble mansion for himself; which makes a grand appearance, rising on the ruins of a Roman station. Without the presence of the lord, he knew it was in vain to expect reformation. He divided his lands into moderate farms; and built commodious farm-houses. As his lands improved, he raised his rents: and his tenants in proportion found it necessary to increase their labour. Thus he has doubled his own income, and introduced a spirit of industry into the country. These indolent inhabitants of the borders begin now to work like other labourers; and notwithstanding they pay higher rents, live more comfortably: for idleness can never be attended with the comforts of industry.

To bring about this great change, Mr. Graham thinks it necessary to rule his subjects with a rod of iron. While he makes them labourers, he keeps them slaves.— Perhaps indeed the rough manners of the people in those parts, could not easily be moulded by the hand of tenderness.

The feudal idea of vassalage, which has long disappeared in all the internal parts of England, remains here in great force; and throws a large share of power into the hands of the landholder. Mr. Graham's estates, which are very extensive, contain about six hundred tenants; all of whom, with their families, lie in a manner at his mercy for their subsistence. Their time and labour he commands, by their mode of tenure, whenever he pleases. Under the denomination of *boon-days*, he expects, at any time, their personal service; and can, in a few hours, muster the strength of five or six hundred men and horses.

Once he had occasion to call them together on military service. On a supposed injury [*], which, about two years ago, he had done the Scotch borderers by intercepting the salmon in the Esk, a body of three hundred of these people marched down upon him with an intention to destroy his works. He had intelli-

---

[*] I have heard since, that this injury has been proved to be a real one; and that reparation hath been made.

gence of their design, and issuing his precepts, mustered, in a few hours, above four hundred men before his gates, armed as the exigence would allow: and if the Scotch, on finding such superiority, had not retreated, Mr. Graham, who told us the story himself, said he believed, that all the spirit and animosity of ancient times would have revived on this occasion.

In a civil light he acts on as large a scale. His manor-courts are kept with great strictness; in which his attorney, with a jury, sits regularly to try causes; and the tenants are injoined, at the hazard of being turned out of their farms, to bring into these courts every suit under the value of five pounds. Thus he prevents much ill-blood among them, by bringing their disputes to a speedy issue; and giving the quarrel no time to rankle. He saves them also much expence: for a suit, which in the king's courts would at least cost five or six pounds; may in his, be carried through all it's forms for eight-pence.—At Patterdale we found a nominal king. Here we found almost a king in reality.

The works on the Esk, which gave so much offence to the Scotch borderers, deserve more notice. They consisted of a massy head thrown across the river, constructed, at a great expence, of hewn stone. This mole was formed at right angles with the bank; but the floods of the ensuing winter swept it away. It was attempted a second time on the same plan; but was a second time destroyed. Mr. Brindley was then sent for, whose works near Manchester had given him high reputation. He changed the plan; and instead of carrying the mole in a direct line across the river, formed it in a curve, arching against the stream: so that it resists the current, as a bridge does the incumbent weight. This work has stood several very great floods, and seems sufficiently firm*. From the curvature of it's form the fall of the water appears also to more advantage. It now forms a semi-circular cascade, which has a good effect.

The chief end which this work had in view, was a fishery. At this place salmon coops

---

* Since this was written, I am informed, Mr. Brindley's work was destroyed from an unsuspected quarter, when the water was low. On the breaking of a frost, a great quantity of ice coming down the river, and collecting at this stoppage, some of it edged under the looser parts of the foundation, and being pressed on with a continued accession of strength, acted like a wedge, and the whole blew up.

are placed; where all the fish, which enter the Esk, are taken. But besides this, and other purposes of utility, it adds great beauty to the neighbourhood. The Esk, which was before in comparison, a shallow stream, gliding unseen beneath it's banks, is now a noble piece of water, raised to a level with them, and seen to great advantage from the house, and every part of the ground.

It was in this part of the country where that dreadful inundation, from the overflowing of Solway-mofs, destroyed lately so large a district. To see the effects of this, was the object of our next expedition.

Solway-mofs is a flat area, about seven miles in circumference. The *substance* of it is a grofs fluid, composed of mud, and the putrid fibres of heath, diluted by internal springs, which arise in every part. The *surface* is a dry crust, covered with mofs, and rushes; offering a fair appearance over an unsound bottom — shaking under the least pressure. Cattle by instinct know, and avoid it. Where rushes grow, the bottom is soundest. The adventrous passenger therefore, who some-times,

times, in dry feafons, traverfes this perilous wafte to fave a few miles, picks his cautious way over the rufhy tuffocks, as they appear before him. If his foot flip, or if he venture to defert this mark of fecurity, it is poffible he may never more be heard of.

At the battle of Solway, in the time of Henry VIII. Oliver Sinclair was imprudently fet over the Scotch army, which had no confidence in him. A total rout enfued; when an unfortunate troop of horfe, driven by their fears, plunged into this morafs, which inftantly clofed upon them. The tale, which was traditional; was generally believed; but is now authenticated. A man and horfe in compleat armour were lately found by the peat-diggers, in the place, where it was always fuppofed the affair had happened; and are preferved at the houfe of a Scotch baronet, if I miftake not, of the name of Maxwell; as we were informed by a gentleman * of the borders, who affured us he had feen them himfelf. The fkeleton of each was well preferved; and the different parts of the armour eafily diftinguifhed.

* Jofeph Dacre, Efq. of Kirklinton, near Longtown.

Solway-

Solway-mofs is bounded on the fouth by a cultivated, and well-inhabited plain, which declines gently, through the fpace of a mile, to the river Efk. This plain is rather lower than the mofs itfelf, being feparated from it by a breaftwork formed by digging peat, which makes an irregular, low, perpendicular, line of black boundary.

It was the burfting of the mofs through this peat breaftwork, over the plain between it and the Efk, which occafioned that dreadful ruin, which we came hither to explore. —— The more remarkable circumftances, relating to this calamitous event, as we had them on the beft authority, were thefe.

On the 16th of November, 1771, in a dark, tempeftuous night, the inhabitants of the plain were alarmed with a dreadful crafh, which they could in no way account for. Many of them were then abroad in the fields, watching their cattle; left the Efk, which was rifing violently in the ftorm, fhould carry them off. None of thefe miferable people could conceive the noife they heard to proceed from any caufe, but the overflowing of the river in fome fhape, tho to them unaccountable. Such indeed, as lived nearer the fource of the eruption, were

fenfible,

ſenſible, that the noiſe came in a different direction; but were equally at a loſs for the cauſe.

In the mean time the enormous maſs of fluid ſubſtance, which had burſt from the moſs, moved ſlowly on, ſpreading itſelf more and more, as it got poſſeſſion of the plain. Some of the inhabitants, through the terror of the night, could plainly diſcover it advancing, like a moving hill. This was in fact the caſe; for the guſh of mud carried before it, through the firſt two or three hundred yards of it's courſe, a part of the breaſtwork; which, tho low, was yet ſeveral feet in perpendicular height. But it ſoon depoſited this ſolid maſs; and became a heavy fluid. One houſe after another, it ſpread round — filled — and cruſhed into ruin; juſt giving time to the terrified inhabitants to eſcape. Scarce any thing was ſaved; except their lives: nothing of their furniture: few of their cattle. Some people were even ſurprized in their beds, and had the additional diſtreſs of flying naked for ſafety.

The morning-light explained the cauſe of this amazing ſcene of terror; diſcovering the calamity in it's full extent: and yet, among all the conjectures of that dreadful night, the

miſchief

mischief which really happened, had never been supposed. Who could have imagined, that a breastwork, which had stood for ages, should give way? or that those subterraneous floods, which had been bedded in darkness, since the memory of man, should burst from their black abode?

This dreadful inundation, tho the first shock of it was the most tremendous, continued still spreading for many weeks, till it covered the whole plain — an area of five hundred acres; and, like molten metal poured into a mould, filled all the hollows, lying in some parts thirty or forty feet deep, reducing the whole to one level surface. The overplus found it's way into the Esk; where it's quantity was such, as to annoy the fish; no salmon, during that season, venturing into the river. We were assured also, that many lumps of earth, which had floated out at sea, were taken up, some months after, at the isle of Man.

As we descended from the higher grounds to take a nearer view of this scene of horror, it exhibited a very grand appearance. The whole plain was covered by a thick smoke, occasioned by a smothering fire set to it in various parts, with a view to consume it; and brought before us that simple, and sublime idea of *the smoke of a country going up like the smoke of a furnace.*

When we came to the plain on that side, which is next the Esk, it had so forbidding an aspect, as far as we could discover through the smoke, that we almost despaired of crossing to the chasm, as we had intended. On horseback it was impossible; and when we had alighted, we stood hesitating on the brink, whether it were prudent, even on foot, to attempt so dangerous a march.

While we remained in this situation, we observed several groups of peasants working in the ruins; and beckoning to the nearest, one of the group came forward. He was an elderly man, strengthening his steps with a long measuring wand. His features, and gait, tho hard and clownish, were marked with an air of vulgar consequence. As he approached, one of our company, who knew him, accosted him by the name of Wilson; and we found he was the person who conducted the works which were set on foot to clear the soil of this melancholy incumbrance.

On informing him of our difficulties, and asking, whether we might venture acrofs the plain; he bad us, like Cæsar, with an air of affurance, follow him, and fear nothing. From one tuffock to another we followed, fometimes ftepping — fometimes leaping — and fometimes hefitating, whether to go on, or to return. In very difficult places our guide condefcended to lay us a plank. In the midft of our perplexity, one of our company, ftraying a ftep from the right path, fell in; but the mud being fhallow in that part, he fank only to the knees. Mr. Wilfon helped him out; but reprimanded his careleffnefs. The reproof and the example having a good effect upon us all, we followed our guide, like packhorfes in a ftring, and at length compleated our undertaking.

When we got to the gulph, from whence all this mifchief had iffued, the fpectacle was hideous. The furface of *the mofs itfelf* had fuffered little change. Near the chafm it appeared indented, through a fpace of feveral yards: but not in any degree as one fhould have expected from fo vaft a difcharge. The mouth of the chafm was heaped round with monftrous piles of ruin, formed by the broken

breaft-

breaſtwork, and ſhell of the moſs, on the firſt great burſt; and a black, moſſy tincture continued ſtill to iſſue from it. If this continue to run, as it probably will, it may be a fortunate circumſtance; and ſave the country from any farther miſchief, by draining this bloated maſs through a perpetual diſcharge.

As we ſtood on the higher ground, and got to windward of the ſmoke, we obtained a clear idea of the plain, and of the courſe of the irruption over it. Many fragments of a very large ſize, which had been carried away in the firſt full ſtream of the diſcharge, appeared thrown to a conſiderable diſtance. Theſe were what made that moving bulwark, which ſome of the inhabitants had ſeen in the night. Fragments of a ſmaller ſize, (and yet many of theſe conſiderable) appeared ſcattered over the plain, as the heavy torrent was able to carry them. The interſtices between the fragments, which had been filled with fluid moſs, were now baked by the heat of the ſun, and cruſted over like the great ſurface of the moſs itſelf. Here and there, along this ſurface, the broken rafters of a houſe, or the top of a blaſted tree were ſeen; and made an odd appearance, riſing as it were, out of the ground, in which they were

were half funk. But through the whole waste, there was not the least sign left of any culture; tho this plain had once been the pride of the country. Lands, which in the evening would have let for twenty shillings an acre, by the morning-light were not worth six-pence.

On this well cultivated plain twenty-eight families had their dwellings, and little farms; every one of which, except a few, who lived near the skirts of it, had the world totally to begin again. Mr. Graham, agreeably to the prudential maxims he has ever observed, affords them little assistance himself; and discourages the bounty of others. He seems to wish his dominions should thrive by industry alone; and would have his subjects depend on this great virtue for the supply of every want, and the reparation of every loss. If the maxim, in so full an extent, be good; it requires at least, a great hardiness of resolution to carry it into practice.

Whether the immense work of clearing this plain can ever totally be effected, is a doubt with many. It is attempted however with great spirit, through the united force of the two powerful elements of fire and water.

All

All the skirts, and other parts of it which are drier than the rest, are reduced by fire; which occasioned the great smoke from the plain, as we descended into it; and which, at that distance, appeared to arise from the whole area.

But this method is not found very effectual; as it reaches only a little below the surface. Much more is expected from the application of water; which is the part our guide Mr. Wilson has undertaken.—How well qualified he is for the undertaking, and in what manner he proposes to accomplish it, may be conceived from the following story.

Mr. Graham's house stands on an eminence, with higher grounds above it. A little on one side of the front, stood a knoll, which made a disagreeable appearance before his windows.— Being desirous therefore of removing it, he sent to Newcastle for a person accustomed to works of this kind. The undertaker came, surveyed the ground, and estimated the expence of moving so much earth, at thirteen hundred pounds.

While the affair was in agitation, Mr. Graham heard, that Wilſon had ſaid, the earth might be removed at a much eaſier rate. He was examined on the ſubject; and his anſwers appeared ſo rational, that he was ſet to work. He had already ſurveyed the higher grounds, where he firſt collected all the ſprings he found, into two large reſervoirs; from which he cut a precipitate channel, pointed at an abrupt corner of the knoll. He cut alſo a channel of communication between his two reſervoirs. Theſe being both filled, he opened his ſluices, and let out ſuch a continued torrent of water, (the upper pool feeding the lower) that he very ſoon carried away the corner of the knoll, againſt which he had pointed his artillery. He then charged again, and levelled againſt another part with equal ſucceſs. In ſhort, by a few efforts of this kind, he carried away the whole hill; and told Mr. Graham, with an air of triumph, that, if he pleaſed, he would carry away his houſe next. The work was compleated in a few days; and Mr. Graham himſelf informed us, that the whole expence did not amount to twenty pounds.

This man, with ſo much genius about him, lives in the loweſt ſtile of life; and works for the lowest wages. When we regretted, that he was paid so inadequately to his worth, we were assured, as his appearance indeed testified, that he had no higher idea of happiness, than to get drunk after his day's labour: and that better wages would only destroy him sooner.

I have since heard, that one hundred and fifty acres of the plain are now cleared by the ingenuity of this man: and that there is reason to believe, he will in time still clear a more considerable quantity. From a reservoir formed by a little stream at the highest part of the overflowed ground, he cuts channels in various directions to the Esk: and when the water is let off, he places numbers of men by the side of each stream, who roll into it large masses of mossy earth, which had been hardened by the sun. The stream tumbles them into the river; and the river conveys them to the sea.

SECT. XXIII.

HAVING feen fuch parts of the country on the borders of England, as were moſt curious; we ſet out on our return. But inſtead of taking the Keſwick-road, we propoſed to vary our rout by the mountains of Brugh*.

At Penrith the road divides. We turned to the left, towards Appelby; and ſoon fell into a rich, and beautiful vale, in which the river Lowther, gliding under lofty woody banks, bore us company a confiderable way.

When we croſſed that river, the fituation of Brougham-caſtle, one of the feats of the

---

* See page 168, vol. 1.

cele-

celebrated countefs of Pembroke, attracted our notice. It had not efcaped the notice of the Romans; who fixed here a ftation to command the country. It appears as great, at this time, in a picturefque light, as it did formerly in a military one. But we had not time to ride up to it; contenting ourfelves with viewing it only as the ornament of a fecond diftance.

At Clifton the road opens again into a wild fcene. Here we examined the fpot, where, in the year 1745, the rebels entering an inclofed country, made a ftand; and lined the hedges to retard the duke of Cumberland's purfuit. Sir Jofeph York, in his road from Ireland, had been there, we found, a few days before. He had accompanied the duke in his expedition againft the rebels; and ftopped at Clifton to review the fcene. He left the people, we were informed, much pleafed with his remembering a gallant action, which had been achieved, about that time, by a heroine of the country, who had carried a letter acrofs the fire of the rebels, when no other meffenger could be obtained.

From

From Clifton, we turned aside to see Lowther-hall, the seat of Sir James Lowther. It is only a temporary house, the old mansion having been burnt in the time of the late lord Lonsdale. But materials are now collecting for a grand structure. It is situated in an extensive park, which contains a great variety of beautiful scenery.

From Lowther-hall we pursued our rout to Appelby, keeping on our left that vast tract of barren country, called Wingfield-forest.

The situation of Appelby-castle, which belongs to the earl of Thanet, is magnificent. It stands on a rocky eminence, falling precipitately into the river Eden; which half incircles it. The banks of the river, and the sides of the precipice, are finely hung with wood. The castle is still in good repair; and is a noble pile. But, in a picturesque light, it loses half it's beauty, from it's being broken into two parts. A *smaller* break from a grand pile removes heaviness; and is a source of beauty. We have seen the principle exemplified in mountains, and other objects*. But here the whole is divided into two parts, of such *equal* dimensions, that each aspires to pre-eminence. Each therefore becomes a separate whole: and both together distract the eye. The detached part should always observe a due inferiority. But what is said of these two detached parts of the castle, is meant only with regard to that view of it, which appears *from the road*. If you go *round it*, you are presented with other views, in which it is seen more advantageously; particularly where you see the bridge, and the first opening into the vale of Eden. There the castle takes a very grand situation on a hanging rock over the river; and the *detached part* makes but an *inconsiderable* appearance.

We had not time to take a view *from* the castle; which must command a beautiful distance, over the vale.

Appelby-castle was the Apallaba of the Romans; and preserves it's origin clearer in it's etymology, than the generality of Roman stations.

---

* See page 55, vol. ii.

This

This castle was formerly the favourite mansion of Ann countess of Pembroke, Dorset, and Montgomery. As this very extraordinary lady is still the object of great veneration in these parts: as her history is curious, and less known than it ought to be; and as it is so intimately connected with all this country; I thought the following digression a proper one.

She was the daughter of George Clifford, earl of Cumberland; one of the heroes of the gallant age of Elizabeth. This noble person distinguished himself chiefly by his naval expeditions; on which he was suffered, in those frugal times, to expend a great portion of his patrimony. In return for his patriotism, he was appointed by his royal mistress, her champion in all tilts and tournaments; where the grace, and dignity of his behaviour, and his skill and address in arms, were equally admired. The rich armour he wore, on these occasions, is still shewn in this castle.

Lady Ann-Clifford was only ten years of age, when her father died. But her education was conducted by two excellent women—

her mother, a daughter of the earl of Bedford — and afterwards by her aunt the countess of Warwick.

In her early youth she married lord Buckhurst, earl of Dorset; with whom during a few years she lived very happily*. But he soon leaving her a widow; she married, six years after, Philip earl of Pembroke, and Montgomery.

This nobleman, through the favour of James I. possessed, as a reward for his great skill in the arts of hunting, and hawking, a prodigious estate; not less, at that time, than eighteen thousand pounds a year. His manner of living was sumptuous beyond example; and his apparatus for field-sports magnificent beyond belief. His dog-kennels were superb; and his stables vied with palaces. But his falconry was his chief pride; which he had furnished, at a wonderful expence, with birds of game; and proper persons to manage, train and exercise them.

Here ends the history of Philip earl of Pembroke — unless we add, that in private

---

* I have seen some accounts, which speak of this marriage as an unhappy one.

life, he was vicious, ignorant, and unlettered in a surprizing degree, and that in public, his character is stained with ingratitude, and tergiversation, by the noble historian of those unfortunate times.

With this worthless man his unhappy lady lived near twenty years. During the latter part of his life indeed he became so dissolute, that she was obliged to leave him.

About the time of his death she found herself possessed of a very ample fortune. For, it seems, her immediate succession to the large estates of her ancestors in the north, had been disputed by an uncle, who inherited the title: and an award had been given against her by James I. to which however she would not submit. But the uncle, and his son both dying, the great estates of the Cliffords, tho considerably impaired by her father's generosity, came to her without any farther molestation. She had besides two large jointures. That which she received from her first husband, was between three, and four thousand, a year; and that from the earl of Pembroke was nearly equal to it.

On the event of the earl of Pembroke's death, she immediately laid out the whole plan of her future life; determining to retire into the north; and spend it on her own estate.

In ancient times the earls of Cumberland possessed five noble castles in the three counties of Yorkshire, Westmoreland, and Cumberland —— Skipton — Pendragon — Appelby — Brougham — and Brugh. The tower of Bardon also was another fortified seat, where they sometimes resided. But all these castles had suffered in the late civil wars; and were reduced, more or less, to a state of great decay.

The countess of Pembroke however determined, on her coming into the north, to repair and furnish them all. This great work she compleated during the years 1657, and 1658; and placed over the gate of each castle the following inscription:

THIS CASTLE WAS REPAIRED BY THE LADY ANN CLIFFORD, COUNTESS DOWAGER OF PEMBROKE, &c. IN THE YEAR —— AFTER THE MAIN PART OF IT HAD LAIN RUINOUS EVER SINCE 1648, WHEN IT WAS DEMOLISHED, ALMOST TO THE GROUND BY THE PARLIAMENT THEN SITTING AT WESTMINSTER, BECAUSE IT HAD BEEN A GARRISON IN THE CIVIL WARS. IS. LVIII. 12. LAUS DEO!

Oliver Cromwell was, at this time, at the head of affairs; whose hypocrisy and villany

the

the countefs of Pembroke detefted: and as fhe had too much fpirit to conceal her fentiments, it is probable, the protector was enough informed, how little fhe efteemed him. Her friends therefore, knowing the jealoufy of his temper, advifed her not to be fo profufe in building; as they were well affured, that as foon as fhe had built her caftles, he would order them to be deftroyed. But fhe anfwered with great fpirit, " Let him deftroy them if he will: but he fhall furely find, that as often as he deftroys them, I will rebuild them, while he leaves me a fhilling in my pocket."

She fhewed her contempt for Cromwell, and her own high fpirit, on another occafion. Her uncle had left her affairs fo involved, that fhe found herfelf under a neceffity of recovering fome of her rights by a tedious lawfuit. The affair being reprefented to Cromwell by the oppofite party, he offered his mediation. But fhe anfwered loftily, fhe would never accept it, while there was any law to be found in England. " What! faid fhe, does he imagine, that I, who refufed to fubmit to king James, will fubmit to him?"

But

But notwithstanding her spirit, neither her castles, nor her estates were injured. Some ascribed this lenity to Cromwell's reverence of her virtue; which is very improbable: others, to her numerous friends, with whom the protector wished to keep fair; which, it is most likely, was the truth.

Her dislike to Cromwell was not founded on party; but on principle. She had the same dislike afterwards to Charles, when she became acquainted with the spirit of his government. On being pressed by her friends, sometime after the restoration, to go to court; " By no means, said she; unless I may be allowed to wear blinkers*."

Besides her castles, she found likewise in ruins, almost all the churches, belonging to the several villages on her estates. The spire of one had been beaten down: another had been turned into a magazine: a third into a hospital. Seven of them were in this ruinous condition: each of which she either built from the ground, or repaired; furnish-

---

* Blinkers are those blinds affixed to the bridles of coach-horses, which prevent their seeing what they ought not to see.

ing them all with decent pews; that her tenants, in every part of her eſtates, might have churches in their neighbourhood.

Her ſeveral buildings, and repairs, at her firſt coming into the north, did not coſt her leſs, than forty thouſand pounds.

At each of her caſtles ſhe reſided a part of every year; regularly moving from one to the other; over-looking the whole of her vaſt eſtates; and bleſſing the country, wherever ſhe went. She was every where the common patroneſs of all, who were diſtreſſed. Her heart was as large, as her ability: and miſery of every kind, that could get it's ſtory fairly repreſented to her, was ſure of relief.

Nor was ſhe content with *occaſional* acts of charity; but made many of her charitable intentions *permanent* by endowments. The greateſt of theſe works were two hoſpitals, which ſhe founded.

One little pleaſing monument of this kind ſtands by the ſide of the road, between Penrith and Appelby. It is a monument indeed rather of her filial piety, than of her charity. On this ſpot, in her early youth, ſhe had parted with her beloved mother; whom ſhe never afterwards ſaw. She always remembered

bered this parting-fcene with the tendereft feelings; and, when fhe came to refide in Weftmoreland, fhe raifed, among her other buildings a pillar to record it; with a ftone-table at it's bafe. The pillar, which is ftill known in the country by the name of *Countefs-pillar*, is decorated with her arms; a fun-dial, for the benefit of travellers; and the following infcription.

THIS PILLAR WAS ERECTED IN THE YEAR 1656, BY ANN COUNTESS DOWAGER OF PEMBROKE, &c. FOR A MEMORIAL OF HER LAST PARTING, IN THIS PLACE, WITH HER GOOD AND PIOUS MOTHER, MARGARET, COUNTESS DOWAGER OF CUMBERLAND, ON THE 2d OF APRIL 1616. IN MEMORY WHEREOF SHE HATH LEFT AN ANNUITY OF £4 TO BE DISTRIBUTED TO THE POOR OF THE PARISH OF BROUGHAM, EVERY 2d DAY OF APRIL FOR EVER, UPON THE STONE TABLE PLACED HARD BY. LAUS DEO!

Her very houfe-hold was a noble charity. Her fervants were generally the children of her tenants; and were fure of a provifion, if they behaved well. Her women-fervants had always little portions given them, to begin the world with, if they married to pleafe her.

The calamities of the times also, during Cromwell's government, particularly the distressed situation of several ejected ministers of the church, furnished her with ample opportunities of exerting her generosity. Among others, she was particularly kind to King, afterwards bishop of Chichester; and Duppa, and Morley, both afterwards bishops of Winchester. To each of these she allowed £40 a year; and when, in their distresses abroad, they informed her, that a sum of money would be of more service to them, than the annuities she was pleased to give them; she remitted a thousand pounds to be divided among them.

She was a lady of uncommon prudence in the management of her affairs. Bishop Rainbow sums up her character on this head, in two words, by calling her a perfect mistress of *forecast*, and *aftercast*.

For the numberless acts of bounty, that flowed from her, she depended, under God, on two things — her regularity in keeping accounts; and her great economy.

With regard to the former, in whatever castle she resided, an office was kept, in which all her receipts, and disbursements were entered

tered with commercial exactness. Of her private charities, she kept an account herself; but was so regular, that, at any time by comparing it with her public accounts, she had, at once, a compleat view of the situation of her affairs.

Her economy was equal to her exactness. Nothing was spent in vanity. Nothing was trifled away. All her family-expences were under the article of necessaries: and the very form of regularity, in which they constantly ran, made one year a check upon another.

The spirit, which she shewed in defending her rights, may perhaps be mentioned also among her plans of economy. It was a spirit not often exerted; but when it was raised, it always carried her vigorously to the end of the question; and, no doubt, secured her from many contentions, which might otherwise have disturbed her, in the midst of so complex a property; and in those dubious days, when legal rights were so much unhinged. I have mentioned her spirit, in one suit, with regard to an affair of consequence. We have an account of another, tho of less importance.

It

It was a custom, on all her estates, for each tenant to pay, besides his rent, an annual *boon-hen*, as it was called. This had ever been acknowledged a just claim; and is, I believe, to this day, paid on many of the great estates in the north; being generally considered as a steward's perquisite.

It happened, that a rich clothier from Halifax, one Murgatroyd, having taken a tenement near Skipton, was called on by the steward of the castle for his *boon-hen*. On his refusal to pay it, the countess ordered a suit to be commenced against him. He was obstinate; and she determined; so it was carried into length. At last she recovered her hen; but at the expence of £200.—— It is said, that after the affair was decided, she invited Mr. Murgatroyd to dinner; and drawing the hen to her, which was served up as the first dish, " Come, said she, Mr. Murgatroyd, let us now be good friends: Since you allow the hen to be dressed at my table, we'll divide it between us."

She had a mind improved, and cultivated in many parts of learning. Dr. Donn, in his humorous manner, used to say, *she knew how to converse of every thing; from predestination*

nation to flea-filk *. But hiftory feems to have been her chief amufement; to the ftudy of which fhe was probably firft led, by examining the hiftory of her own anceftors. This indeed comprehended, in a great degree, the hiftory of England from the times of the conqueft: for there were few fcenes of public life, in which her progenitors, the Veteriponts and the Cliffords, an active race of men, were not deeply engaged.

She feems to have entertained a defign of collecting materials for a hiftory of thefe two potent northern families. At a great expence fhe employed learned men to make collections, for this purpofe, from the records in the tower; the rolls; and other depofitaries of public papers; which being all fairly tranfcribed, filled three large volumes. This work, which contains anecdotes of a great variety of original characters, exerting themfelves on very important occafions, is ftill, I have heard, among the family-records at Appelby-caftle.

While fhe was thus careful to preferve the honour of her anceftors; fhe inftituted a very

---

* A kind of raw filk ufed, at that time, in embroidery.

severe historical restraint, if I may so call it, on herself. In a large folio volume, which made a part of her equipage, when she travelled from one castle to another, she ordered an entry to be made, under her own inspection, of the transactions of every day. To what particulars this journal extended, I have not learned. But if it was kept, as it probably was, by a confidential secretary, it might have included very minute particulars. What an interesting collection of valuable anecdotes might be furnished from the incidents of such a life! What a satire would it be on the vanity, the dissipation, and frivolous employments of the generality of the great! This work, I am informed, is still extant; and in the hands of the earl of Thanet *.

But the most conspicuous part of the character of this illustrious lady, was her piety and great attachment to religion. No doubt the amiable instructors of her youth had given her disposition, naturally serious, a proper

---

* I have since been informed, that the late earl of Thanet destroyed it, as it contained many severe remarks on several characters of those times, which the earl supposed might give offence to their families.

direction: but perhaps the best school, in which she had learned to think justly, was, that school of affliction, the house of her second husband, the earl of Pembroke; whose dissipated, abandoned life had taught her, more than any thing else, the vanity of all earthly things, unless used for the purposes they were given.

Few divines were better versed in scripture, than she was. She could quote it pertinently on all occasions; and never failed to read a portion of it every day; or have it read to her, in the latter part of her life.

The new testament was her principal study. Next to it she was particularly fond of the psalms of David; and had those appointed for the day, read regularly to her.

She had been bred up in the church of England from her youth; and tho' she could not, in the fanatical times of the usurpation, attend any public service; yet in the worst of those times she never failed to hear the church-service in her own private chapels, which she had been careful to fit up in all her castles. Many menaces of sequestrations she received from the ruling powers, if she persisted in that practice. But she shewed the same spirit on this occasion, which she
had

had before shewn on many others. She continued her practice; and left them to do as they pleased. No attempts however were made against her.

She had no idea of pomp, and grandeur. With regard to herself, her mode of living was rather parsimonious. Amidst all the objects of her generosity, herself was the only person forgotten. In her diet she was even abstemious; and would sometimes pleasantly boast, that she had scarce ever tasted wine, or physic; during her whole life. Of the elegance of dress she had never been fond; but in her latter life she laid it intirely aside; wearing nothing, for many years, but a close habit of plain, black serge; which occasioned many pleasant mistakes between her, and her attendants.

Her retinue was merely for use, not parade. Besides her common domestics, she had always two ladies of education, who lived with her. Many hours she spent alone: at other times, they read to her, and were her companions.

Her chief expence, as far as concerned herself, was in books. Her library was stored with all the best writers in the English language. She knew no other.

Such was the life of this excellent lady; equally suited to any station, in which God had pleased to place her. It was a life of no more indulgence, than the most abridged circumstances would have allowed. Her ability in doing good, was that only, in which she exceeded others.

She lived twenty-six years, after the death of her second husband; Providence lengthening out her life, as a blessing to the country, beyond her eightieth year. The 23d of March 1675 was the day of her dissolution — one of the most melancholy days the northern counties ever experienced.

In her ended the noble family of the Cliffords. Her daughter Margaret, by the earl of Dorset (her sole surviving heiress) marrying the earl of Thanet, carried the Clifford estates into the Tufton family *.

---

* The most material part of this little history is taken from a MS. life of Mr. Sedgwick, her secretary, written by himself. In this work Mr. Sedgwick occasionally inserts a few circumstances relating to his lady. — It is a pity he had not given her the better share. His MS. is still extant in Appelby-castle.

SECT.

SECT. XXIV.

FROM Appelby-castle we soon approach the barrier-mountains: but we approach them, in the usual order of nature, by regular progress. The ground is first high, before it becomes mountainous; and tillage appears in scanty plots, before cultivation ceases.

A little to the north of Brugh, the ground on the left, makes a singular appearance. A hill, on which a fair is annually held, forms an exact, semi-circular convex. Scarce a knoll, or bush breaks the regularity of the line. Beyond this, but without any intervening ground, rises a range of distant mountains. These wore a light purple hue, when we saw them — the circular hill, a deep green. Perhaps no disposition of ground was ever more totally

totally unpicturesque: and yet even this (such is the force of contrast) it it be only bisected, and in a small degree adorned, is not wholly disagreeable.

At the commencement of the mountains stand the town, and castle of Brugh, not unpleasantly seated. The castle which consists, like that at Appelby, of two parts, seems to have been a very strong place. Since the time of it's last noble inhabitant, the countess of Pembroke, it has been falling fast into ruin; but we found it no easy matter, even yet, to scale the out-works of it's earthern mounds: so strong a fortress hath it once been. — Some parts of it, especially a shattered round tower, are very picturesque.

We had not the opportunity of seeing this castle in so advantageous a light, as had favoured us, when we saw the castle of Penrith. We saw them both in the evening; but here we had no bright beam of sun-set to *illumine the ruins*. And yet the effect was grand. The castle and landscape around, were in deep shadow; under the influence of a retiring storm, which had hung a settled gloom on all
the

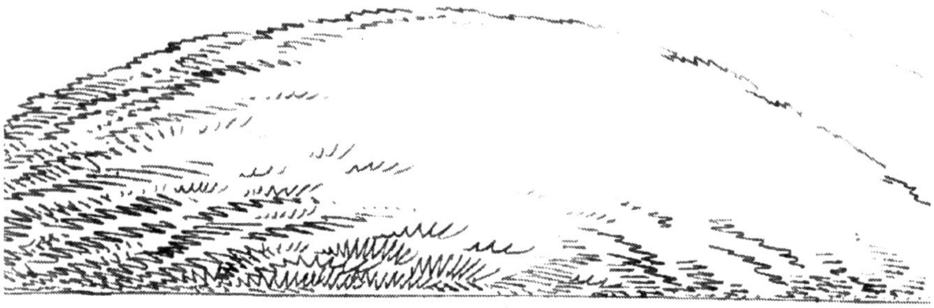

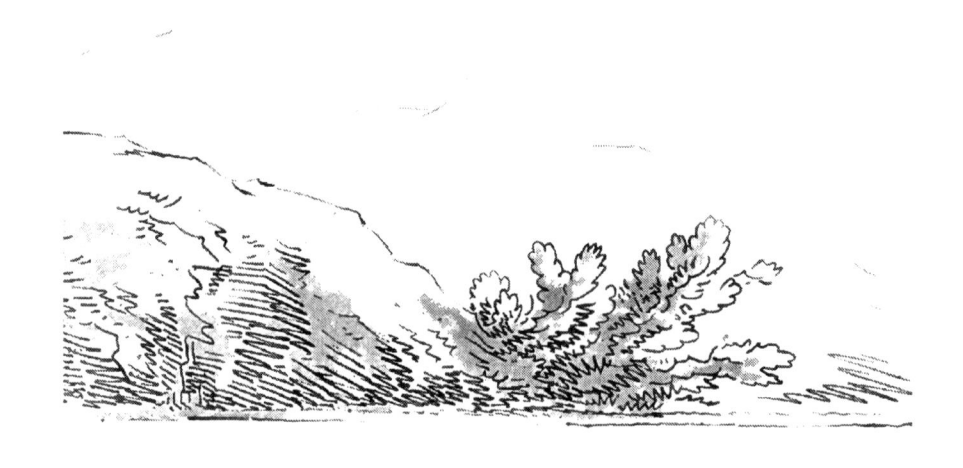

the upper regions of the sky. The sun was invisible; but had fired the whole western horizon with a deep red. We viewed the castle from the east; and had therefore the ruddy part of the hemisphere as a background to the grey tints, and strong shadows of the towers, and battlements, which intervened between us and the west. These, with the deep solemnity of the gloom, were a sufficient balance to the glowing red of the horizon, which would otherwise have been too glaring. But the whole was in perfect harmony; and had a fine effect. — Indeed nature's *colouring* is rarely without harmony. If the lights be glowing, the shades are proportionably deep; on the contrary, if the lights decay, the shadows decay with them; and as light is also the source of colour, the landscape wears always one uniform hue. Either the *sober colouring* prevails, or one *vivid tint* supports another. In *composition* *, we have found, that nature may be improved; but in the beauty, and proportion of *her tints*, in the harmony of her *colouring*, she is seldom at variance with herself.

---

* See the idea of improving natural composition, explained, p. 125, &c. vol. 1.

The square tower, which made the grand part of the castle, conveyed, as we looked into it, a very horrid idea. Most of these old structures have suffered great *external* dilapidations. But here the *shell* was intire; and all the *internal* parts were gone — the roof, the stories, and even the vault over the dungeon. The whole was a mere excavation. I know not, that I was ever struck with a more horrid idea of the kind. The eye, confined within the walls of a vast tower, open to the sky above, which loured with unusual blackness, looked down with hideous contrast, deep into a dungeon below.

The whole road, over the mountains of Stainmore, from Brugh-castle to Bowes-castle, which is about thirteen miles, is the most unpleasant that can be conceived; and the more so, as it reminded us of the sublime scenes, which we had passed, in another part of this chain, between Amblesíde and Kefwick. In the mountains of Stainmore, the parts are neither sufficiently ample to be grand; nor
rich

rich and varied, to be beautiful. We did not even find what we have elfewhere called *a mere fcene of mountains* *. In fuch a fcene, the *parts* are beautiful, tho there is no *whole*; but here, in a picturefque view, there is neither *whole*, nor *parts*.

Nothing remains of Bowes-caftle, but one heavy, fquare tower, much defaced, and ruined; tho the ftone-work appears to have been excellent. This fortrefs feems originally to have been intended as a defence at the fouthern end of the mountains; as Brugh-caftle was at the northern.

From the pofition of thefe caftles, it feems probable, that formerly the road over the mountains of Stainmore was the only road into Cumberland, that was paffable, and of courfe neceffary to be defended. The Kefwick mountains, till lately, were impervious; and the mountains of Shap are much fuller of defiles, and dangerous paffes, than thofe of Stainmore, which are the moft level, and the moft penetrable part of this vaft chain.

---

* See page 168, vol. I.

As we leave the mountains, a very rich and extensive view opens before us into Yorkshire. We had not seen such a view for many days. For tho in Cumberland, we had many very extensive prospects, yet they extended chiefly over barren country.

At Greta we found much devastation from the late high floods. The bridge was beaten down; and large fragments of it carried away, through the violence of the stream. With these, and huge stones torn from the adjoining cliffs, the bed of the river was choaked. Nothing could have a more ruinous appearance. A *broken bridge* impresses one of the strongest emblems of desolation, from the idea of cutting off all intercourse among men.

Here sir Thomas Robinson has a house[*], situated in a pleasant park; one side of which is bounded by the river.

---
[*] It is now Mr. Morritt's.

The road from Greta-bridge leads through a rich country, but open, and unpleasing; unless in distance.

The middle of Gatherly-moor commands a most extensive view in every direction. Hambledon-hills bound the prospect in front. On the right stretches an extent of country towards Richmond. A distance still more remote opens, on the left, into the bishopric of Durham; and behind rise the mountains of Westmoreland, as a background to all the wild scenes we had left.

Few places afford a situation, where a painter may see, at once, so many *modes of distance:* or where he may better compare, at one glance, their several beauties and imperfections.

The wild, unwooded waste, when thrown into distance, hath neither variety, nor richness. It is one uniform, dark, and dreary spread: unless it be happily inlightened; or consist of hilly ground broken into large parts.

The intermixture of tracts of woodland, adds a pleasing variety to distance; and is adapted to receive the sweetest effects of light.

But

But the cultivated country forms the moſt amuſing diſtance*. Meadows, corn-fields, hedge-rows, ſpires, towns, and villages, tho loſt as *ſingle objects*, are all melted together into the *richeſt maſs of variegated ſurface*; over which the eye ranges with delight; and following the flitting gleams of ſun-ſhine, catches a thouſand dubious objects, as they ariſe; and creates as many more, which do not really exiſt. But ſuch a country will not bear a nearer approach; eſpecially if it be over-built, which is the caſe of moſt of the rich diſtances about London: the *parts* aſſume too much conſequence, and the *whole* becomes a ſcene of confuſion.

When the death of Elizabeth called James to the crown of England, he took this road from Scotland; and on Gatherly-moor, we are told, he ſtopped to take a view around him; with which he is ſaid to have been greatly delighted. The ſpot, where this royal ſurvey was taken, is ſtill ſhewn — the ſummit of a Roman ſtation. — It is not likely, that

---
* See page 7, vol. 1.

picturesque

picturefque thoughts engaged his princely attention at that time. It is rather probable, that he began there to meafure the length of his new fceptre — for there his wiftful eyes were bleffed with the firſt fair profpect of the promifed land.

From Gatherly-moor we entered Leeming-lane; grieved to leave fo much fine country on both fides unfeen. Within a few miles the Tees pouring through a rocky channel, forms fome of the moft romantic fcenery in England; and boafts, at Winfton-bridge, a more magnificent fingle arch, than perhaps any Englifh river can produce. — Within a few miles, in another direction, lie the beautiful, and varied grounds about Richmond; which among other noble fcenes, exhibit the magnificent ruins of a caftle, on the fummit of a lofty rock, over-hanging the Swale.——— All this beautiful country we were obliged to leave behind, and enter Leeming-lane, which extends near thirty miles, in a ftraight line, fhut up between hedges; being a part of a great Roman caufey. And yet the whole is fo well planted, that we found it lefs difgufting, than

we

we expected. The smallest turn, where the wood hung loosely over the lane, especially when there was any variety in the ground, broke the lines, and destroyed much of the disagreeable regularity of the road.

We left the lane however abruptly, and went to Norton Conyers, near Rippon, the seat of sir Bellingham Graham; from whence we proposed to visit the neighbouring scenes of Studley, and Hackfall.

SECT. XXV.

THE moſt improved part of the gardens at Studley, and what is chiefly ſhewn to ſtrangers, is a valley, nearly circular, ſurrounded by high woody grounds, which ſlope gently into it in various directions. The circumference of the higher grounds includes about one hundred and fifty acres; the area, at the bottom, conſiſts of eight. The higher parts preſent many openings into the country. The lower, of courſe, are more confined; but might afford many pleaſing woody ſcenes, and ſolitary retreats. A conſiderable ſtream runs through the valley: and on the banks of this ſtream, in another valley, contiguous to the circular one, ſtand the ruins of Fountain's abbey; the grandeſt, and moſt beautiful, except perhaps thoſe of Glaſtonbury, which the kingdom can produce.

The idea, which such vallies naturally suggest, is that of retirement — the habitation of chearful solitude. Every object points it out; all tending to soothe and amuse: but not to rouse and transport; like the great scenes of nature.

Sometimes indeed the recluse may be more enamoured of the great scenes of nature, and wish to fix his abode, where his eye may be continually presented with sublime ideas. But in general, we observe (from the whole history of monastic life) that he wishes rather to sequester himself in some tranquil scene: and this in particular was chosen as a quiet recess, consecrated to retirement.

Solitude therefore being the reigning idea of the place, every accompaniment should tend to impress it. The ruins of the abbey, which is the great object, certainly do. The river and the paths should wind carelessly through the lawns and woods, with little decoration. Buildings should be sparingly introduced. Those which appear, should be as simple as possible — the mere retreats of solitude. The scene allows no more; and the neighbourhood of so noble a ruin renders every other

other decoration, in the way of building, either trivial, or offensive.

Instead of these ideas, which the vallies of Studley naturally suggest, the whole is a vain ostentation of expence; a mere *Timon's villa*; decorated by a taste debauched in it's conception, and puerile in it's execution. Not only the reigning idea of the place is forgotten; but all the great master-strokes of nature, in every shape, are effaced. Every part is touched and retouched with the insipid sedulity of a Dutch master:

—— Labor improbus omnia vincit.

What a lovely scene might a person of pure taste have made at Studley, with one tenth part of the expence, which hath been laid out in deforming it.

Fresh shadows fit to shroud from sunny ray;
Fair lawns to take the sun in season due;
Sweet springs, in which a thousand nymphs did play;
Soft, tumbling brooks, that gentle slumber drew;
High reared mounts, the lands about to view;
Low-winding dales, disloigned from common gaze;
Delightful bowers to solace lovers true.

Such might have been the scenes of Studley; but such is the whimsical channel of human operations,

operations, that we sometimes see the pencil of Reubens employed on a country wake; and that of Teniers disgracing the nuptials of an emperor.

On the whole, it is hard to say, whether nature has done more to embellish Studley; or art to deform it. Much indeed is below criticism. But even, where the rules of more genuine taste have been adopted, they are for the most part unhappily misapplied. In the point of opening views, for instance, few of the openings here are simple, and natural. The artifice is apparent. The marks of the sheers, and hatchet, are conspicuous in them all. Whereas half the beauty of a thing consists in the easiness of it's introduction. Bring in your story awkwardly; and it offends. It is thus in a view. The eye roving at large in quest of objects, cannot bear prescription. Every thing forced upon it, disgusts; and when it is apparent, that the view is *contrived*; the *effect is lost*.

The valley, in which Fountain's abbey stands, is not of larger dimensions, than the other, we have just described: but instead of the circular form, it winds (in a more beautiful proportion) into length. It's sides are
composed

composed of woody hills sloping down in varied declivities; and uniting with the trees at the bottom, which adorn the river.

At one end of this valley stand the ruins of the abbey, which formerly overspread a large space of ground. Besides the grand remains of ruin, there appeared in various parts, among the trees and bushes, detached fragments, which were once the appendages of this great house. One of these, which was much admired, seemed evidently to have been a court of justice.

Such was the general idea of this beautiful valley, and of the ruins which adorned it, before they fell into the hands of the present proprietor. Long had he wished to draw them within the circle of his improvements: but some difficulties of law withstood. At length they were removed; and the time came (which every lover of picturesque beauty must lament) when the legal possession of this beautiful scene was yielded to him; and his busy hands were let loose upon it.

A few fragments scattered around the body of a ruin are *proper*, and *picturesque*, They are *proper*, because they account for what is defaced: and they are *picturesque*, because they unite the principal pile with the ground; on which union the beauty of composition, in a good measure, depends*. But here they were thought rough and unsightly; and fell a sacrifice to neatness. Even the court of justice was not spared; tho a fragment, probably as beautiful, as it was curious.

In the room of these detached parts, which were the proper and picturesque embellishments of the scene, a gaudy temple is erected, and other trumpery wholly foreign to it.

But not only the scenery is defaced, and the outworks of the ruin violently torn away; the main body of the ruin itself, is, at this very time, under the alarming hand of decoration.

The remains of this pile are very magnificent. Almost the intire skeleton of the abbey-church is left, which is a beautiful piece of Gothic architecture. The tower seems wholly to have escaped the injuries of time. It's mouldering lines only are softened. Near the church stand a double row of cloysters; which

---

* See the same idea in mountains, p. 50, vol. ii. and in building, p. 146, and afterwards in cattle, Sect. XXXI.

are singularly curious from the pointed arches, which do the office of columns, in supporting the roof. At the end of these cloysters stand the abbot's apartments; which open into a court, called the Monk's garden. On one side of this court is the hall, a noble room; which communicates, in the spirit of hospitality, with the kitchen. There are besides a few other detached parts.

When the present proprietor made his purchase, he found this whole mass of ruin, the cloysters, the abbey church, and the hall, choaked with rubbish. His first work therefore was to clear and open. And *something* in this way, might have been done with propriety. For we see ruins sometimes so choaked, that no view of them can be obtained.

To this business succeeded the great work of *restoring*, and *ornamenting*. This required a very delicate touch. Among the ruins were found scraps of Gothic windows; small, marble columns; tiles of different colours; and a variety of other ornamental fragments. These the proprietor has picked from the rubbish with great care; and with infinite industry is now restoring to their old situation. But in vain;

vain; for the friability of the edges of every fracture, makes any restoration of parts an awkward patchwork.

Indeed the very idea of giving a finished splendor to a ruin, is absurd. How unnatural, in a place, evidently forlorn and deserted by man, are the *recent* marks of human industry! — Besides, every sentiment, which the scene suggests, is destroyed. Instead of that soothing melancholy, on which the mind feeds in contemplating the ruins of time; a sort of jargon is excited by these heterogeneous mixtures; as if, when some grand chorus had taken possession of the soul — when the sounds in all their sublimity, were yet vibrating on the ear — a light jig should strike up.

But the *restoration* of parts is not enough; *ornaments* must be added: and such incongruous ornaments, as disgraced the *scene*, are disgracing also the *ruin*. The monk's *garden* is turned into a trim parterre, and planted with flowering shrubs: a view is opened, through the great window, to some ridiculous figure, (I know not what; Ann Bolein, I think, they called it) that is placed in the valley; and in the central part of the abbey-church, a circular pedestal is raised out of the fragments of the
old

old pavement; on which is erected — a mutilated heathen statue!!!

It is a difficult matter, at the sight of such monstrous absurdities, to keep resentment within decent bounds. I hope I have not exceeded. A *legal* right the proprietor unquestionably has to deform his ruin, as he pleases. But tho he fear no indictment in the king's bench, he must expect a very severe prosecution in the court of taste. The refined code of this court does not consider an elegant ruin as a man's *property*, on which he may exercise at will the irregular sallies of a wanton imagination: but as a deposit, of which he is only the guardian, for the amusement and admiration of posterity. — A ruin is a sacred thing. Rooted for ages in the soil; assimilated to it; and become, as it were, a part of it; we consider it as a work of nature, rather than of art. Art cannot reach it. A Gothic window, a fretted arch, some trivial peculiarity may have been aimed at with success: but the *magnificence* of ruin was never attained by any modern attempt.

What reverence then is due to these sacred relics; which the rough hand of temerity, and caprice dare mangle without remorse? The least error is irretrievable. Let us pause a moment.—— A Goth may deform: but it exceeds the power of art to amend.

The scenes of Studley, which I have here described, are confined to the two contiguous vallies. The improvements of the place extend considerably farther: but we had neither time, nor inclination, to examine more. We had seen enough.

About the close of the last century, a piece of human antiquity existed in the neighbourhood of this abbey, still more curious, than the abbey itself — that venerable instance of longevity, Henry Jenkins. Among all the events, which, in the course of a hundred and sixty-nine years, had fastened upon the memory of this singular man, he spoke of nothing with so much emotion, as the ancient state of Fountain's abbey. If he were ever questioned on that subject, he would be sure to inform you,
" What

"What a brave place it had once been;" and would speak with much feeling of the clamour, which it's diffolution occafioned in the country*. "About a hundred and thirty years ago, he would fay, when I was butler to lord Conyers, and old Marmaduke Bradley, now dead and gone, was lord abbot, I was often fent by my lord to inquire after the lord-abbot's health; and the lord abbot would always fend for me up into his chamber, and would order me roaft-beef †; and waffel; which I remember well, was always brought in a *black-jack*." —— From this account we fee what it was that rivetted Fountain's abbey fo diftinctly in the old man's memory. The *black-jack*, I doubt not, was a ftronger idea, than the fplendor of the houfe, or the virtues of the lord-abbot.

---

* The *fubftance* of thefe particulars the author had from a MS fhewn him by fir Bellingham Graham.

† The MS. fays, *a quarter of a yard* of roaft-beef. I have heard that the monafteries ufed to meafure out their beef; but in what way I never underftood.

SECT.

SECT. XXVI.

FROM Studley we visited the scenes of Hackfall. These own the same proprietor; and are adorned with equal taste.

It is a circumstance of great advantage, to be carried to this grand exhibition (as you always should be) through the *close lanes* of the Rippon road. You have not the least intimation of a design upon you, nor any suggestion, that you are on high grounds; till the folding-doors of the building at Mowbray-point being thrown open, you are struck with one of the grandest, and most beautiful bursts of country, that the imagination can form.

Your eye is first carried many fathoms precipitately down a bold, woody steep, to the river Ewer, which forms a large semi-circular curve

curve below; winding to the very foot of the precipice, on which you ſtand. The trees of the precipice over-hang the central part of the curve.

In other parts too the river is intercepted by woods; but enough of it is diſcovered to leave the eye at no uncertainty in tracing it's courſe. At the two oppoſite points of the curve, two promontories ſhoot into the river, in contraſt with each other: that on the right is woody, faced with rock, and crowned with a caſtle: that, on the left, riſes ſmooth from the water, and is ſcattered over with a few clumps. The peninſular part, and the grounds alſo at ſome diſtance beyond the iſthmus, con- ſiſt of one intire woody tract; which ad- vancing boldly to the foot of the precipice, unites itſelf with it.

This woody ſcenery on the banks of the river may be called the firſt diſtance. Beyond this lies a rich, extenſive country — broken. into large parts — decorated with all the ob- jects, and diverſified with all the tints of diſtant landſcape — retiring from the eye, ſcene after ſcene — till at length every vivid hue fading gradually away, and all diſtinction of parts being loſt, the country imperceptibly

melts

melts into the horizon; except where the blue hills of Hambledon clofe the view.

Through the whole extent of this grand fcene — this delightful gradation of light and colours — nature has wrought with her broadeft, and freeft pencil. The parts are ample: the compofition perfectly correct. She hath admitted nothing difgufting, or even trivial. I fcarce remember any where an extenfive view fo full of beauties, and, at the fame time, fo free from faults. Nothing difgufts. The foreground is as pleafing as the background; which it never can be, when plots of cultivation approach the eye: and it is rare to find fo large an extent of near-ground, covered by wood, or other furface, whofe parts are alike grand, and beautiful.

The vale, of which this view is compofed, hath not yet intirely loft it's ancient name — the *vale of Mowbray*; fo called from Mowbray-caftle now no longer traced even in it's ruins; but once fuppofed to be the capital manfion of thefe wide domains. This vale extends from York almoft to the confines of Durham; is adorned by the Swale, and the Ewer, both confiderable rivers; and is certainly

tainly one of the noblest tracts of country of the kind in England.

Hackfall is as much a contrast to Studley, as the idea of *magnificence* is to that of *solitude*. It requires of course a different mode of ornament. A banqueting house, inriched with every elegance of architecture, in the form perhaps of a Grecian temple, might be a proper decoration at Mowbray-point; which at Studley would be superfluous, and absurd. The ruins of a castle too, if they *could* be executed with veri-similitude and grandeur, might adorn the rocky promontory on the right with propriety. The present ruin is a paltry thing. Any other ornamental building, besides these two, I should suppose unnecessary. These might sufficiently adorn every part of the scenery, both in the higher, and in the lower grounds. If the expence, which is generally laid out, in our great gardens, on a variety of *little* buildings, was confined to one or two *capital objects*, the general effect would be better. A profusion of buildings is one of the extravagances of false taste. *One* object is a proper ornament in every scene: more than

than one, at least on the foregrounds, distract it. Particular circumstances indeed may add a *propriety* to a greater number of objects: as at Kew; where a specimen is given of different kinds of religious structures: or at Chiswick; where it is intended to exhibit an idea of various modes of architecture. But it is *unity* of *design*, not of *picturesque composition*, which pleases in these scenes. As far as this is concerned, one handsome object is enough.

Having examined the whole of this very extraordinary burst of landscape from Mowbray-point, we descended to the bottom, where a great variety of grand, and pleasing views are exhibited; particularly a view of Mowbray-point from Limus-hill; and another of the promontory with the castle upon it, from the tent: and it must be acknowledged, that many of these views are opened in a very natural, and masterly manner. If any art hath been used, it hath been used with discretion.

At the same time, amidst all this profusion of great objects, and all this grandeur of *design*

sign (for nature has here not only brought her materials together, but has compofed them likewife) the eye is every where called afide from the contemplation of them by fome trivial object — an awkward cafcade —a fountain — a view through a hole cut in a wood — or fome other ridiculous fpecimen of abfurd tafte.

It is a great happinefs however, that the improver of thefe fcenes had lefs in his power at Hackfall, than he had at Studley. The vallies there, and home-views were all within the reach of his fpade, and axe. Here he could only contemplate at a diftance what glorious fcenes he might have difplayed, if his arm could have extended to the horizon. Some of the nearer grounds of this grand exhibition, (I believe all beyond the Ewer,) are the property of another perfon. So that the whole peninfular part, and the grounds immediately beyond it, continue facred, and untouched: and thefe are the fcenes, which form the grand part of the view from Mowbray-point. In furveying thefe, the eye overlooks the *puerilities of improvement* at the bottom of the precipice.

The banks of rivers are fo various, that I know not any two river-views of any celebrity, which at all refemble each other in the *detail*; tho in the *general caſt, and outlines* of the fcene, they may agree. Thus at Studley, and at* Corby, the materials of the fcenery are, in both places, the fame. Each hath it's woody banks — it's river — and the ruins of an abbey. In each alfo the beauties of the fcene are in a great meafure fhut up in a valley within itfelf; and the idea of folitude is impreffed on both. Notwithftanding this fimilarity, two fcenes can hardly be more different. At Corby, the woody bank is grander than that at Studley, bordering rather on the fublime. At Studley, the form and contraft of the vallies, and the great variety of the ground, is more pleafing. In the former fcene the river is fuperior: in the latter, the ruins. In one, you wander about the mazes of a circular woody bank: in the other, the principal part of the walk is continued along the margin of the river; the

---

* See page 102.

woody bank, which is too steep to admit a path, serving only as a skreen.

There is the same union and difference between the scenes of Persfield*, and Hackfall. Both are *great* and *commanding* situations. The river, in both, forms a *sweeping curve*. Both are adorned with *rocks, and woods:* and sublimity is the reigning idea of each. Notwithstanding all these points of union, they are wholly unlike. Persfield, tho the country is open before it, depends little on it's beauties. It's own wild, winding banks supply an endless variety of rocky scenery; which is sufficient to engage the attention. The banks of Hackfall are less magnificent; tho it's river is more picturesque, and it's woods more beautiful. But it's views into the country are it's pride; and beyond any comparison, grander and more inchanting, than those at Persfield.

From Hackfall we returned to our hospitable quarters at *Norton Conyers*, which is

---

* See observations on the Wye, page 39:

situated

situated in a pleasant park-scene; but too flat to admit much variety.

In the time of the civil wars, the owner of this mansion was Sir Richard Graham; of whom we heard an anecdote in the family, which is worth relating; as it is not only curious in itself, but throws a very strong, and yet natural shade, on the character of Cromwell.

When the affairs of Charles I. were in their wane in all the southern counties; the marquifs of Newcastle's prudence gave them some credit in the north. His residence was at York, where he engaged two of the gentlemen of the country to act under him as lieutenants. Sir Richard Graham was one; whose commission under the marquifs is still in the hands of the family. As Sir Richard was both an active man, and much attached to the royal cause; he entered into it with all that vigour, which ability, inspired by inclination, could exert; and did the king more effectual service, than perhaps any private gentleman in those parts.

On that fatal day, when the precipitancy of prince Rupert, in opposition to the sage advice of the marquifs, led the king's forces out of York againſt Cromwell, who waited for them on Marſden-moor, Sir Richard Graham had a principal command; and no man did more than he, to end an action with fuccefs, which had been undertaken with temerity.

When the day was irretrievably loſt; and nothing remained, but for every man to feek the beſt means of fecurity that offered, Sir Richard fled, with twenty-fix bleeding wounds upon him, to his own houſe at Norton Conyers, about fifteen miles from the field. Here he arrived in the evening: and being fpent with lofs of blood, and fatigue, he was carried into his chamber; where taking a laſt farewell of his difconfolate lady, he expired.

Cromwell, who had ever expreſſed a peculiar inveteracy againſt this gentleman, and thought a victory only half obtained, if he efcaped; purfued his flight in perfon, with a troop of horfe.

When he arrived at Norton, his gallant enemy was dead; having fcarce lived an hour, after he was carried into his chamber: and Cromwell found his wretched lady weeping

over

over the mangled corpse of her husband, yet scarce cold.

Such a sight, one should have imagined, might have given him — not indeed an emotion of pity — but at least a satiety of revenge. The inhuman miscreant still felt the vengeance of his soul unsatisfied; and turning round to his troopers, who had stalked after him into the sacred recesses of sorrow, he gave the sign of havoc; and in a few moments the whole house was torn to pieces: not even the bed was spared, on which the mangled body was extended: and every thing was destroyed, which the hands of rapine could not carry off.

In this country we met with another curious memorial of the battle of Marsden-moor. A carpenter, about two years ago, bought some trees, which had grown there. But when the timber was brought to the saw-pit, it was found very refractory. On examining it with more attention, it appeared, that great numbers of leaden bullets were in the hearts of several of the trees; which thus recorded the very spot, where the heat of the battle had raged.

SECT. XXVII.

FROM Norton we propofed to take our rout, through Yorkfhire into Derbyfhire and fo through the other midland counties into the fouth of England.

The town of Rippon makes a better appearance, as you approach it, than the generality of country towns. The church is a large building; and gives a confequence to the place.

From Rippon the road is not unpleafant; paffing generally through a woody country, till we entered Knarefborough-foreft, where all wood ceafed. Like other royal chafes, it hath now loft all it's fylvan honours, and is a wild, bleak, unornamented tract of country.

Near the close of the forest, lies Harrogate, in the dip of a hill; a cheerless, unpleasant village. Nor does the country make any change for the better; till we cross the river Wharf.

From hence, leaving the ruins of Harewood-castle on the left, and Harewood-house on the right, we ascended, by degrees, a tract of high ground, and had an extensive view which was illumined, when we saw it, by those gleaming, cursory lights, which are so beautiful in distant landscape; and so common, when the incident of a bright sun, a windy sky, and floating clouds coincide. It is amusing, under these circumstances, to pursue the flitting gleams, as they spread, decay, and vanish — then rise in some other part; varied by the different surfaces, over which they spread.

We have this appearance beautifully detailed in an old Erse poem, the title of which is Dargo. The bard poetically, and picturesquely

resquely compares the short transitions of joy in the mind, to these transitory gleams of light.

"The tales of the years that are past, are beams of light to the soul of the bard. They are like the sun-beams, that travel over the heaths of Morven. Joy is in their course, tho darkness dwells around. Joy is in their course; but it is soon past: the shades of darkness pursue them: they overtake them on the mountains; and the footsteps of the chearful beam are no longer discovered. — Thus the tale of Dargo travels over my soul like a beam of light, tho the gathering of the clouds is behind."

We should have been glad to have examined Harewood-house, as it is a sumptuous pile; but it is shewn only on particular days; and we happened to be there on a wrong one.

We regretted also another misfortune of the same kind, for which we had only ourselves to blame; and that was the omission of Kirkstall-abbey. In the precipitancy of an an early morning, and through an unaccountable error in geography, we paſſed it; and did not recollect the miſtake, till we were half a day's journey beyond it.

Around Leeds the ſoil wears an unpleaſant hue; owing in part to the dirtineſs of the ſurface; within a few yards of which, coal is every where found. — The country however changes greatly for the better, before we arrive at Wakefield, which lies in the midſt of beautiful ſcenery. The river Calder makes a fine appearance, as we leave the town; and it's banks are adorned by a Gothic chapel, now in ruins, dedicated by Edward IV., to the memory of the duke of York, his father, and the other chiefs of his party, who fell at the battle of Wakefield. It is built in the elegant proportion of ten by ſix; plain on the ſides; but richly adorned on the front; and finiſhed with a ſmall octagon turret at the eaſt end. — This little edifice ſerves both to aſcertain the hiſtory of architecture, which appears to have been near it's meridian; and to illuſtrate an important part of the Engliſh ſtory. It's whimſical ſituation by the ſide of of a bridge, was intended probably to mark the spot, where some principal part of the action happened: tho at the entrance of great towns it was not unusual, in popish times, to place chapels on bridges; that travellers might immediately have the benefit of a mass. There was, for this purpose, a chapel formerly in one of the piers of London-bridge.

Not far from Wakefield we rode past a piece of water, which takes the humble name of a mill-pond; but is in fact a beautiful little lake, being near two miles in circumference, and containing some pleasing scenery, along it's little woody shores, and promontories.

From Bank-top we had a good descending view of Wentworth-castle — of the grounds, which inviron it — and the country, which surrounds it. The whole together is grand. The eminence, on which we stood, is adorned with a great profusion of something, in the way of an artificial ruin. It is possible it may have an effect from the castle below; but

but *on the spot*, it is certainly no ornament. We found some difficulty in passing through lord Strafford's park; and proceeded therefore to Wentworth-house; which is a superb; and is esteemed, an elegant pile: but there seems to be a great want of simplicity about it. The front appears broken into too many parts; and the inside, incumbered. A simple plan has certainly more dignity. Such, for instance, is lord Tilney's house at Wanstead, where the whole is intelligible *at sight*. The hall at lord Rockingham's is a cube of sixty feet. The gallery is what they call a *shelf*. For myself, I saw nothing offensive in it, tho it is undoubtedly a more masterly contrivance to raise a gallery *upon* a wall, than to affix one *to it*. The long gallery is a noble apartment; and the interception of a breakfast room from it by pillars, and an occasional curtain, gives a pleasant combined idea of retirement, and company. The library also is grand.

There are few good pictures at Wentworth. The original of lord Strafford, and his secretary, is said to be here. It's pretensions are disputed; tho I think it has merit enough to maintain them any where. — There is another good

good portrait by Vandyke of the fame nobleman. He refts his hand upon a dog, and his head in this picture is perhaps fuperior to that of the other.—Here is alfo, by Vandyke, a fon of the fame earl, with his two fifters. The management of the whole difpleafes; but the boy is delightfully painted.

Wentworth-houfe ftands low. It's front commands an extenfive plain, and a flat diftant country; which are feen betwixt a rifing wood on the left; and a variety of croffing lawns on the right. On the whole, we were not much pleafed with any thing we faw here.

SECT. XXVIII.

FROM Wentworth-houfe the fame pleafant face of country continues to Sheffield. But it foon begins to change, as we approach Derbyfhire. The rifing grounds become infenfibly more wild: rocks ftart every where from the foil; and a new country comes on apace. For we now approached that great central tract of high lands; which arifing in thefe parts, form themfelves into mountains; and fpreading here and there, run on without interruption, as far as Scotland*. Before we reach Middleton, the whole face of the land has fuffered change; and we fee nothing around us, but wildnefs and defolation.

---

* See page 3, vol. 1.

About two miles ſhort of Middleton we are cheared again by a beautiful valley; which participates indeed of the wildneſs of the country; but is both finely wooded, and watered. In a receſs of this valley ſtands Middleton, a very romantic village; beyond which the valley ſtill continues two miles farther.

It is this *continuation* of it, which is known by the name of Middleton-dale; and is eſteemed one of the moſt romantic ſcenes of the country. It is a narrow, winding chaſm; hardly broader than to give ſpace for a road. On the right, it is rocky; on the left, the hills wear a ſmoother form. The rocks are grey, tinged in many parts with plots of verdure inſinuating themſelves, and running among them. Some of theſe rocks aſſume a peculiar form, rearing themſelves like the round towers, and buttreſſes of a ruined caſtle; and their upper ſtrata running in parallel directions, take the form of cornices. The *turriti ſcopuli* of Virgil cannot be illuſtrated better. I ſhould not however affirm, they are the more pictureſque on this account. Nature's uſual forms, when beautiful in their kind, are generally the moſt beautiful.

When

When we leave Middleton-dale the waftes of Derbyshire open before us; and wear the fame face as thofe we had left behind, on the borders of Yorkshire. They are tracts of coarfe, moorifh pafturage, forming vaft convex fweeps, without any interfection of line, or variation of ground; divided into portions by ftone walls, without a cottage to diverfify the fcene, or a tree to enliven it. Middleton-dale is the pafs, which unites thefe two dreary fcenes.

Having travelled feveral miles in this high country, in our way to Caftleton, we came at length to the edge of a precipice; down which ran a long, fteep defcent. From the brow, an extenfive vale lay before us. It's name is Hope-dale. It is a wide, open fcene of cultivation; the fides of which, tho mountainous, are tilled to the top. The village of Hope ftands at one end of it, and Caftleton at the other. In a direction towards the middle of this vale we defcended. The object of our purfuit, was that celebrated chafm, near Caftleton, called the *Devil's-cave*.

A defcent of two miles brought us to it. — A combination of more horrid ideas is rarely found, than this place affords. It exceeded our livelieft imagination.

A rocky mountain rifes to a great height: in moft parts perpendicular; in fome, beetling over it's bafe. As it afcends, it divides; forming at the top, two rocky fummits. — On one of thefe fummits ftands an old caftle; the battlements of which appear to grow out of the rock. It's fituation, on the edge of a precipice, is tremendous. Looking up from the bottom, you may trace a narrow path, formed merely by the adventrous foot of curiofity, winding here and there round the walls of the caftle; which, as far as appears, is the only road to it. — The other rock referves it's terrors for the bottom. There it opens into that tremendous chafm, called the Devil's-cave. Few places have more the air of the poetical regions of Tartarus.

The combination of a caftle, and a cave, which we have here in *reality*, Virgil *feigns* — with a view perhaps of giving an additional terror to each.

——— Æneas

——— Æneas arces, quibus altus Apollo
Præsidet, horrendæque procul secreta Sibyllæ,
Antrum immane, petit ———

The poet does not give the detail of his *antrum immane*: if he had, he could not have conceived more interesting circumstances, than are here brought together.

A towering rock hangs over you; under which you enter an arched cavern, twelve yards high, forty wide, and near a hundred long. So vast a canopy of *unpillared* rock stretching over your head, gives you an involuntary shudder. A strong light at the mouth of the cave, displays all the horrors of the *entrance* in full proportion. But this light decaying, as you proceed, the imagination is left to explore it's deeper caverns by torch-light, which gives them additional terror. At the end of the first cavern runs a river, about forty feet wide, over which you are ferried into a second, of dimensions vaster than the first. It is known by the name of the Cathedral. The height of it is horribly discovered by a few spiracles at the top; through which you see the light of the day, without being able, at such a distance, to enjoy the least benefit from it. It may be called a kind of star-light. Beyond this cavern flows another branch of the fame river which becomes the boundary of other caverns still more remote. But this was farther than we chose to proceed. I never found any picturesque beauty in the interior regions of the earth; and the idea growing too infernal, we were glad to return

——— cœli melioris ad auras.

The inhabitants of these scenes are as savage as the scenes themselves. We were reminded by a disagreeable contrast of the pleasing simplicity and civility of manners, which we found among the lakes and mountains of Cumberland. Here a wild, uninformed stare, through matted, dishevelled locks, marks every feature; and the traveller is followed, like a spectacle, by a croud of gazers. Many of these miserable people live under the tremendous roof we have just described; where a manufacture of rope-yarn is carried on. One poor wretch has erected a hut within it's verge, where she has lived these forty years. A little straw suffices for a roof, which has only to resist the droppings of unwholesome vapour from the top of the cavern.

The exit from Hope-dale, in our road to Buxton, is not inferior to the scene we had left. We ascend a straining steep, ornamented on each side, with bold projecting rocks, most of which are picturesque; tho some of them are rather fantastic.

As we leave this pass, on our right appears *Mam-tor*, surnamed the *Shivering mountain*. A part of it's side has the appearance of a cascade; down which it continually discharges the flaky substance, of which it is composed.

On the confines of this mountain, and but a little below the surface, is found that curious, variegated mineral, which is formed into small ornamental obelisks, urns and vases. It is supposed to be a petrifaction; and is known in London by the name of the *Derbyshire drop*. But on the spot it is called *Blue John*, from the blue veins, which overspread the finest parts of it. Where it wears a yellowish hue, the vein is coarsest: in many parts it is beautifully

tifully honeycombed, and tranfparent. The proprietors of the marble works at Afhford farmed the quarry of this curious mineral, laft year, at ninety-five pounds; and it is thought have nearly exhaufted it.

From Hope-dale to Buxton, the country is dreary, and uncomfortable. The eye ranges over bleak waftes, fuch as we had feen before, divided every where by ftone walls. The pafturage in many parts feems good, as the fields were ftocked with cattle; but hardly a tree, or a houfe appears through the whole diftrict.

In a bottom, in this uncomfortable country, lies Buxton, furrounded with dreary, barren hills; and fteaming, on every fide, with offenfive lime-kilns. Nothing, but abfolute want of health, could make a man endure a fcene fo wholly difgufting.

Near Buxton we vifited another horrid cave, called *Pool's hole*; but it wants thofe magnificent accompaniments of *external* fcenery, which we found at the Devil's-cave.

The fame dreary face of country continues from Buxton to Afhford. Here we fall into a beautiful vale fringed with wood, and watered by a brilliant ftream, which recalled to our mememory the pleafing fcenes of this kind we had met with among the mountains of Cumberland.

At Afhford is carried on a manufactory of marble dug on the fpot; fome of which, curioufly incrufted with fhells, is very beautiful.

The vale of Afhford continues with little interruption to Bakewell, where it enters another fweet vale — the vale of Haddon; fo called from Haddon-hall, a magnificent old manfion, which ftands in the middle of it, on a rocky knoll, incompaffed with wood.

This princely ftructure, fcarce yet in a ftate of ruin, is able, it is faid, to trace it's origin into times before the conqueft. It then wore a military form. In after ages, it became poffeffed possessed by different noble families; and about the beginning of this century was inhabited by the dukes of Rutland. Since that time, it has been neglected. Many fragments of it's ancient grandeur remain — sculptured chimnies; fretted cornices, patches of costly tapestry;

Auratasque trabes, veterum decora alta parentum.

Not far from hence lies Chatsworth, in a situation naturally bleak; but rendered not unpleasant by the accompaniments of well-grown wood.

Chatsworth was the glory of the last age, when trim parterres, and formal water-works were in fashion. It *then* acquired a celebrity, which it has never lost, tho it has *now* many rivals. A good approach has been made to it; but in other respects, when we saw it, it's invirons had not kept pace with the improvements of the times. Many of the old formalities remained. But a dozen years, no doubt, have introduced much improvement.

The house itself would have been no way striking; except in the wilds of Derbyshire. The chapel is magnificent. It is adorned, on
the

the whole of one fide, by a painting in frefco, reprefenting Chrift employed in works of charity.

There are few pictures in the houfe. A portrait of the late duke of Cumberland by Reynolds was the beft. But there is much exquifite carving by the hand of Gibbons. We admired chiefly the dead fowl of various kinds, with which the chimney of one of the ftate rooms is adorned. It is aftonifhing to fee the downy foftnefs of feathers given to wood. The particulars however alone are admirable: Gibbons was no adept at compofition.

From Chatfworth, through Darley-dale, a fweet, extenfive fcene, we approached Matlock.

The rocky fcenery about the bridge is the firft grand fpecimen of what we were to expect.

As we advanced towards the boat-houfe, the views became more interefting.

Soon after the *great Torr* appeared, which is a moft magnificent rock, decorated with wood, and ftained with various hues, yellow, green, and grey. — On the oppofite fide, the rocks, contracting the road, flope diagonally.

Thefe ftraits open into the vale of Matlock; a romantic, and moft delightful fcene, in which

the

the ideas of sublimity and beauty are blended in a high degree. It extends about two miles in length; and in the widest parts is half a mile broad. The area consists of much irregular ground. The right hand bank has little consequence, except that of shaping the vale. It is the left hand bank which ennobles the scene. This very magnificent rampart, rising in a semi-circular form, is divided into four ample faces of rock, with an interruption of wood between each. The first, which you approach, is the highest; but of least extent: the next spreads more; and the third most of all. A larger interruption succeeds; and the last, in comparison of the others, seems but a gentle effort. The whole rampart is beautifully shaded with wood; which in some places, grows among the cliffs, garnishing the rocks — in others, it grows wildly among those breaks, and interruptions, which separate their several faces. The *summit* of the whole semi-circular range is finely adorned with scattered trees, which often break the hard lines of the rock; and by admitting the light, give an airiness to the whole.

The river Derwent, which winds under this semi-circular screen, is a broken, rapid stream. In some places only, it is visible: in others, delving among rocks, and woody projections, it is an object only to the ear.

It is impossible to view such scenes as these, without feeling the imagination take fire. Little fairy scenes, where the parts, tho trifling, are happily disposed; such, for instance, as the cascade-scene * in the gardens at the Leasowes, please the fancy. But this is scenery of a different kind. Every object here, is sublime, and wonderful. Not only the eye is pleased; but the imagination is filled. We are carried at once into the fields of fiction, and romance. Enthusiastic ideas take possession of us; and we suppose ourselves among the inhabitants of fabled times. — The transition indeed is easy and natural, from romantic scenes to romantic inhabitants.

———————— Sylvis scena coruscis
Desuper, horrentique atrum nemus imminet umbra;
Nympharum domus ————

---

* See page 59, vol. i.

The

The woods here are subject to one great inconvenience — that of periodical lopping. About seven years ago, I had the mortification to see almost the whole of this scenery displaying one continued bald face of rock. It is now, * I should suppose, in perfection. More wood would cover, and less would dismantle it †.

The *exit* of this bold romantic scene, (which from the south is the *entrance* into it,) like the exit from Hope-dale, is equal to the scene itself. Grand rocks arise on each side, and dismiss you through a winding barrier, which lengthens out the impression of the scene, like the vibration of a sound. In some parts the solid stone is cut through;

Admittitque viam sectæ per viscera rupis.

---

* In the year 1772.

† This whole side of the river is now, I am told, in the hands of a proprietor who will not allow the wood to be lopped periodically any more. It may however be suffered to become too luxuriant; and efface the rock.

From

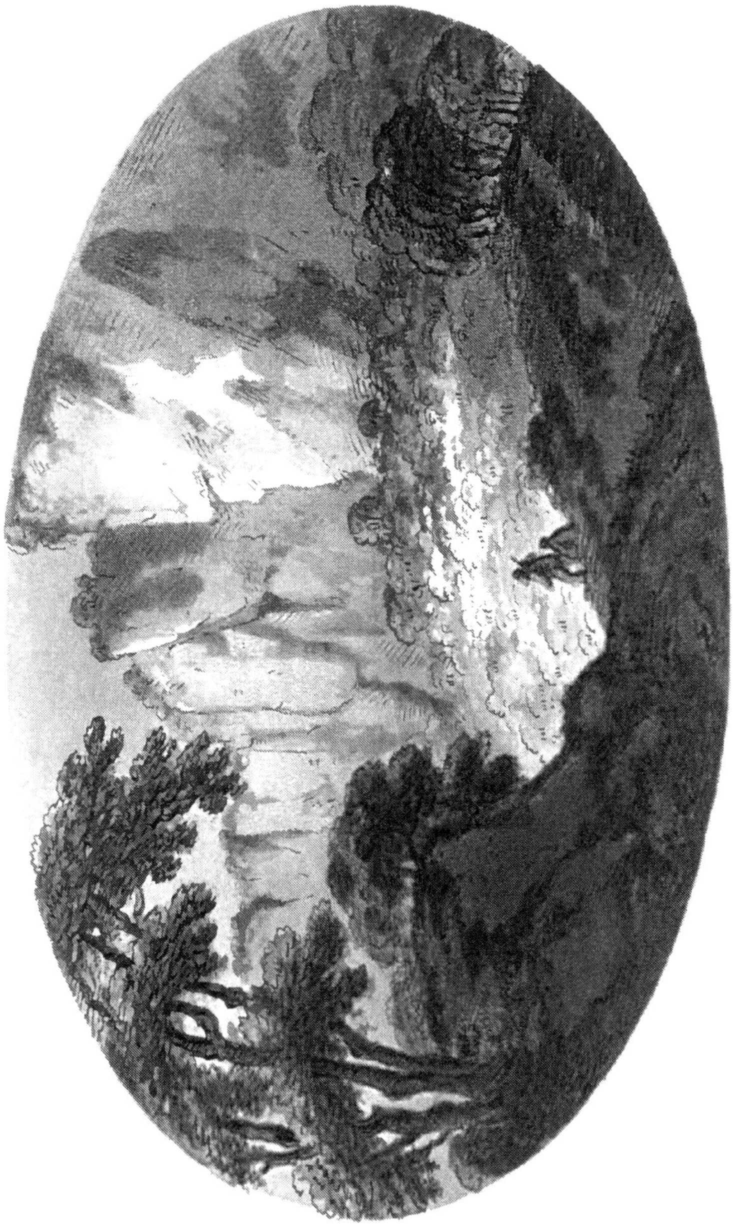

From hence to Ashburn the road is pleasant, after the first steeps. The ground is varied, and adorned with wood; and we lose all those wild scenes, which we met with in the Peak. When nature throws her *wild scenes* into beautiful composition; and decorates them with great, and noble objects; they are, of all others, the most engaging. But as there is little of this decoration in the *wild scenes of the Peak*, we left them without regret.

SECT.

SECT. XXXIX.

FROM Afhburn, which is among the larger villages, and ftands fweetly, we made an excurfion to *Dove-dale*.

Dove-dale is the continuation of another fimilar dale, which is fometimes called *Bunſter-dale*; tho I believe both parts of the valley are known, except juſt on the ſpot, by the general name of Dove-dale.

Bunſter-dale opens with a grand craggy mountain on the right. As you look up to the cliffs, which form the irregular fides of this precipice, your guide will not fail to tell you the melancholy fate of a late dignitary of the church, who riding along the top of it with a young lady, behind him, and purfuing a track, which happened to be only

only a sheep-path, and led to a declivity; fell in attempting to turn his horse out of it. He was killed; but the young lady was caught by a bush, and saved. — A dreadful story is an admirable introduction to an awful scene. It rouses the mind; and adds double terror to every precipice.

The bare sides of these lofty craggs on the right, are contrasted by a woody mountain on the left. In the midst of the wood, a sort of rocky-wall rises perpendicular from the soil. These detached rocks are what chiefly characterize the place. — A little beyond them, we enter, what is properly called, Dove-dale.

From the description given of Dove-dale, even by men of taste, we had conceived it to be a scene rather of curiosity, than of beauty. We supposed the rocks were formed into the most fantastic shapes; and expected to see a gigantic display of all the conic sections. But we were agreeably deceived. The whole composition is chaste, and picturesquely beautiful, in a high degree.

On the right, you have a continuation of the fame grand, craggy mountain, which ran along Bunfter-dale; only the mountain in Dove-dale is higher, and the rocks ftill more majeftic, and more detached.

On the left, is a continuation alfo of the fame hanging woods, which began in Bunfter-dale. In the midft of this woody fcenery arifes a grand, folitary, pointed rock, the characteriftic feature of the vale; which by way of eminence is known by the name of Dove-dale-church. It confifts of a large face of rock, with two or three little fpiry heads, and one very large one: and tho the form is rather peculiar, yet it is pleafing. It's rifing a fingle object among furrounding woods takes away the fantaftic idea; and gives it fublimity. It is the multiplicity of thefe fpiry heads, which makes them difgufting: as when we fee feveral of them adorning the fummits of alpine mountains*. But a *folitary* rock, tho fpiry, has often a good effect. A picturefque ornament of this kind, marks a beautiful fcene, at a place

---

* See page 81, vol. i.

called the *New-Weir*, on the banks of the Wye [*].

The colour of all thefe rocks is *grey*; and harmonizes agreeably with the verdure, which runs in large patches down their channelled fides. Among all the picturefque accompaniments of rocks, nothing has a finer effect in painting, than this variation and contraft of colour, between the cold, grey hue of a rocky furface, and the rich tints of herbage.

The valley of Dove-dale is very narrow at the bottom, confifting of little more than the channel of the Dove, which is a confiderable ftream; and of a foot-path along it's banks. When the river rifes, it fwells over the whole area of the valley; and has a fine effect. The grandeur of the river is then in full harmony with the grandeur of it's banks.

Dove-dale is a calm, fequeftered fcene; and yet not wholly the haunt of folitude, and contemplation. It is too magnificent, and too interefting a piece of landfcape, to leave the mind wholly difengaged.

---

[*] See obfervations on the Wye, page 24.

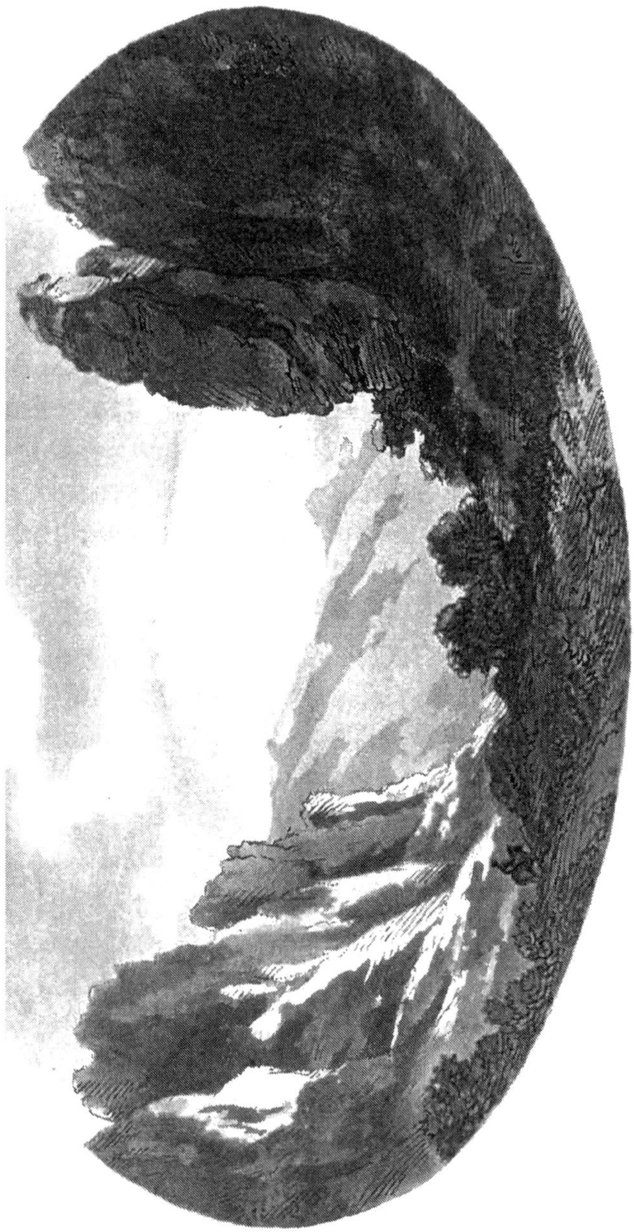

The late Dr. Brown, comparing the scenery here, with that of Keswick[*], tells us, that *of the three circumstances, beauty, horror, and immensity* (by which last he means *grandeur*) *of which Keswick consists, the second alone is found in Dove-dale.*

In this description he seems, in my opinion, just to have inverted the truth. It is difficult to conceive, why he should either rob Dove-dale of *beauty*, and *grandeur*; or fill it with *horror*. If *beauty* consist in a pleasing arrangement of pleasing parts, Dove-dale has certainly a great share of *beauty*. If *grandeur* consist in large parts, and large objects, it has certainly *grandeur* also. But if *horror* consist in the vastness of those parts, it certainly predominates less here, than in the regions of Keswick. The hills, the woods, and the rocks of Dove-dale are sufficient to raise the idea of *grandeur*; but not to impress that of *horror*.

On the whole, Dove-dale is perhaps one of the most pleasing scenes of the kind we any where meet with. It has something in

---

[*] In a letter to lord Lyttelton, already quoted.

it peculiarly characteristic. It's detached, perpendicular rocks stamp it with an image intirely it's own: and for that reason it affords the greater pleasure. For it is in landscape, as in life; we are most struck with the peculiarity of an original character; provided there is nothing offensive in it.

From Dove-dale we proceeded to Ilam; which is another very characteristic scene.

Ilam stands on a hill, which slopes gently in front; but is abrupt, and broken behind, where it is garnished with rock, and hanging wood. Round this hill sweeps a semi-circular valley; the area of which is a flat meadow, nearly a quarter of a mile in breadth, and twice as much in circumference. At the extremity of the meadow winds the channel of a river, considerable in it's dimensions; tho penuriously supplied with water: and beyond all, sweeps a grand, woody bank, which forms a background to the scenery behind the house; and yet, in the front, admits a view of distant mountains; particularly of that square-capt hill, called Thorp-cloud, which stands near the entrance of Dove-dale.

Besides

Besides the *beauty* of the place, we are presented with a great *curiosity*. The river *Manifold* formerly ran in that channel under the woody bank, which we observed to be now so penuriously supplied.—It has deserted it's ancient bed; and about seven miles from Ilam, enters gradually the body of a mountain; under which it forces a way, and continues it's subterraneous rout as far as the hill, on which Ilam stands. There it rises from the ground, and forms a river in a burst. The channel under the bank is a sort of waste-pipe to it; carrying off the superfluity of water, which in heavy rains cannot enter the mountain.

Curious this river certainly is: but were it mine, I should wish much to check it's subterraneous progress, and throw it into it's old channel. The oozy bed, which is nwo a deformity, would then be an object of beauty, circling the meadow with a noble stream.—Another deformity also would be avoided, that of cutting the meadow with two channels.—Or perhaps all ends might be answered, if the waste-stream could be diverted. Then both the curiosity; and, in a good degree, the beauty, would remain.

On the whole, we have few fituations fo pleafingly romantic, as Ilam. The rocky hill it ftands on; the ample lawn, which incircles it; the bold, woody bank, which invirons the whole (where pleafing walks might be formed) the bold incurfion of the river; the views into the country; and the neighbourhood of Dove-dale, which lies within the diftance of an evening walk, bring together fuch a variety of uncommon, and beautiful circumftances, as are rarely to be found in one place.

Very little had been done, at Ilam, when we faw it, to embellifh it's natural fituation; tho it is capable of great improvement; particularly in the front of the houfe. There the ground, which is now a formal flower-garden, might eafily be united with the other parts of the fcenery in it's neighbourhood. It is now totally at variance with it.

In the higher part of the garden, under a rock is a feat dedicated to the memory of Congreve; where, we were told by our conductor, he compofed feveral of his plays.

From Ilam we went to Oakover to see the *holy family* by Raphael. As this picture is very celebrated, we gave it a minute examination.

Whether it be an original, I am not critic enough in the works of Raphael to determine. I should suppose, it is; and it were a pity to rob it of it's greatest merit. Nothing, I think, but the character of the master could give it the reputation it holds. If it be examined by the rules of painting, it is certainly deficient. The manner is hard, without freedom; and the colouring black, without sweetness. Neither is there any harmony in the whole. What harmony can arise from a conjunction of red, blue, and yellow, of which the draperies are composed, almost in raw tints? Nor is the deficiency in the colouring, compensated by any harmony in the light and shade.

But these things perhaps we are not led to expect in the works of Raphael. In them we seek for grace, drawing, character, and expression. Here however they are not found. The virgin, we allow to be a lovely figure:

but Joseph is inanimate; the boys are grinning satyrins; and with regard to drawing, the right arm of Christ, I should suppose, is very faulty [*].

On the whole, a holy family is a subject but indifferently adapted to the pencil. Unless the painter could give the mother that *celestial love*; and the child, that *divine composure*, and *sweetness*, (which, I take it for granted, no painter can give,) the subject immediately degenerates into *a mother*, and *a child*. The *actions* of our Saviour's life may be good subjects for a picture: for altho the divine energy of the principal figure cannot be expressed: yet the other parts of the story being well told, may supply that deficiency. But in a holy family there is *no action*—no story told—the whole consists in the expression of characters and affections, which we

---

[*] Since I made these remarks I was glad to see a kind of sanction given them by a great authority. Sir Joshua Reynolds, in one of his lectures, before the academy, speaks very slightly of the *easel-pictures* of Raphael; which, he says, give us no idea of that great master's genius

muſt ſuppoſe beyond conception. So that if theſe are not expreſſed, the whole is nothing.

In the ſame room hang three or four pictures, any of which I ſhould value more than the celebrated *Raphael*. There is a ſmall picture, by Rubens, repreſenting the angels appearing to the women in the garden, which pleaſed me. The angels indeed are clumſey figures; and dreſſed like choiriſters: but every other part of the picture, and the management of the whole, is good.

In a large picture alſo of the unjuſt ſteward, the family in diſtreſs is well deſcribed: but on the whole, it is one of thoſe ambiguous pictures, on which we cannot well pronounce *at ſight*. One half of it ſeems painted by *Rubens*; of the other half we doubted.

There are alſo in the ſame room two very capital *Vanderveldts* — a calm, and a ſtorm. Both are good: but the former pleaſed me better, than almoſt any picture by that maſter, I have any where ſeen.

SECT. XXX.

FROM Afhburn, to which we returned from Oakover, we went, the next day, through a chearful, woody country, to Keddlefton, the feat of lord Scarfdale.

The fituation of Keddlefton, participates little of the romantic country, on which it borders. The houfe ftands in a pleafant park, rather bare of wood; but the deficiency is in a great degree compenfated by the beauty of the trees; fome of which are large, and noble. A ftream, by the help of art, is changed into a river, over which you are conducted by a good approach obliquely to the houfe.

The architecture of Keddlefton, as far as I could judge, is a compofition of elegance, and grandeur. The main body of the houfe, which you enter by a noble portico, is joined, by a corridore on each fide, to a handfome wing.

wing. In the back-front, the faloon, which is a rotunda, appears to advantage. From the hall lead the ftate rooms, which are not many. The reft of the houfe confifts of excellent offices, and comfortable apartments; and the plan of the whole is eafy, and intelligible.

The hall is perhaps one of the grandeft, and moft beautiful private rooms in England. The roof is fupported by very noble columns; fome of which are intire blocks of marble, dug, as we were informed, from lord Scarfdale's own quarries. It is rather indeed a fpurious fort of marble; but more beautiful, at leaft in colour, than any that is imported. There is a richnefs, and a variety in it, that pleafes the eye exceedingly: the veins are large, and fuited to columns; and a rough polifh, *by receiving the light in one body*, gives a noble fwell to the column; and adds much to it's beauty.

When I faw this grand room, I thought it wanted no farther decoration. All was fimple, great, and uniform, as it ought to be. Since that time I have heard the doors, and windows have been painted, and varnifhed in the cabinet ftyle. I have not feen thefe alterations; and cannot pronounce on their merit: but I am

at

at a lofs to conceive, that any farther embellifhment could add to the effect.

The *entrance* of a great houfe, fhould, in my opinion, confift only of that kind of beauty, which arifes merely from fimplicity and grandeur. Thefe ideas, as you proceed in the apartments, may detail themfelves into ornaments of various kinds; and, in their *proper places*, even into prettineffes. Alien, mifplaced, ambitious ornaments, no doubt, are *every where* difgufting: but in the *grand entrance* of a houfe, they fhould *particularly* be avoided. A falfe tafte, difcovered there, is apt to purfue you through the apartments; and throw it's colours on what may happen to be good. — I fhould be unwilling however to fuppofe, that any improper decorations are added to the hall at Keddlefton; as the ornaments of the houfe, in general, when I faw it, feemed to be under the conduct of a chafte and elegant tafte. Tho every thing was rich; I do not recollect, that any thing was tawdry, trifling, or affected.

The pictures, of which there is a confiderable collection, are chiefly, what may be called good *furniture pictures*[*]. A Rembrandt is

---

[*] See page 24, vol. 1.

the firſt in rank; and is indeed a valuable piece. It repreſents *Daniel interpreting Belteſhazzar's dream.* There is great amuſement in this picture. It is highly finiſhed; and the heads are particularly excellent. For the reſt, it is a ſcattered piece, without any idea of compoſition.

In the drawing-room are two large uprights by Benedetto Lutti; one repreſenting the laſt ſupper; the other the death of Abel. They are painted in a ſingular manner with ſtrong lights. The former has a good effect. The death of Abel is likewiſe a ſhewy picture; but has nothing very ſtriking in it, except the figure of Cain.

In the dead game by Snyders, there is a good fawn; but the picture is made diſagreeable by the *glaring* tail of a peacock.

In the dead game and dogs, by Fyt, there are good *paſſages*, but no *whole*.

The *woman of Samaria*, and *St. John in the wilderneſs*, by B. Stiozzi, are good pictures.

There is alſo a large Coyp, well painted; but badly compoſed.

At

At Derby, which lies within three miles of Keddleston, we were immediatly struck with the tower of the great church, which is a beautiful piece of Gothic architecture.

The object of the china-works there is merely ornament; which is particularly unhappy, as they were, at the time we saw them, under no regulation of taste. A very free hand we found employed in painting the vases; and the first colours were *laid in* with spirit: but in the *finishing*, they were so richly daubed, that all freedom was lost in finery.—It may now be otherwise.

The gaudy painters however of such works, have the example of a great master before them, even Raphael himself; whose paintings in the pottery way, tho highly esteemed in the cabinets of the curious, seem generally to be daubed with very glaring colours. It is said, that Raphael fell in love with a potter's daughter; and that to please her, he painted her father's dishes.

dishes. It is probable therefore, that he suited them to her taste; which accounts for the gaudy colouring they display. — How much more simple, elegant, and beautiful is the painting of the old Etruscan vases, many of which Mr. Wedgewood has so happily imitated? There we see how much better an effect is produced by chaste colours on a dark ground; than by gaudy colours, on a light one.

A person curious in machinery would be much amused by the silk-mill at Derby, in which thirty thousand little wheels are put in motion by one great wheel. The various parts, tho so complicated in appearance, are yet so distinct in their movements; that we were told, any one workman has the power of stopping that part of the machinery, which is under his direction, without interrupting the motion of the rest.

The country between Derby and Leicester is flat. Quardon-wood, a little beyond Loughborough, rising on the right, makes an agreeable variety, amidst such a continuation of uniformity.

uniformity. Mount Sorrel alfo has the fame effect.

The approach to Leicefter gives it more confequence than it really has. The town itfelf, old and incumbered, has little beauty: but it abounds with fragments of antiquity.

Behind St. Nicholas's church is a piece of Roman architecture; one of the only *pure* pieces perhaps in England. We fee many towers, which go by the name of Cæfar; and boaft of Roman origin. I doubt, whether any of them can boaft it with truth. And what few *remnants* we have, it is thought, have all been retouched in after times. This fragment feems to have fuffered no alteration. It's infignificance has fecured it. Little more is left, than a wall, with four double arches on it's face, retiring, but not perforated. And yet in this trifling remnant there is a fimplicity and dignity, which are very pleafing. It is poffible however that prejudice may in part, be the fource of it's beauty. Through an affociation of ideas, we may here be pleafed with what we have admired in Italian views.— This wall is built of brick; tho it has probably been faced with better materials. For what purpofe it was conftructed, does not appear: nor whether it was intended for the end, or fide of a building. The idea of the country is, that it has been a temple, from the great number of bones of animals, which have been found near it: from whence it takes the name of *Holy-bones.*

The church of St. Nicholas, which ftands oppofite to it, feems to have been built out of it's ruins, from the many Roman bricks with which it abounds. Indeed the ftyle of building, in the body of the church, is not unlike it.

At Leicefter alfo we were put on the purfuit of another Roman fragment — a curious piece of fculpture; which we found at laft in a cellar. It is a fcrap of teffulated pavement, on which three figures are reprefented; a ftag; a woman leaning over it; and a boy fhooting
with

with a bow. It may be a piece of Roman antiquity; but it is a piece of miferable workmanfhip.

In this ancient town are found alfo many veftiges of Britifh antiquity. — From fo rich an endowment as the abbey of Leicefter formerly poffeffed, we expected many beautiful remains; as it is ftill in a kind of fequeftered ftate: but in that expectation we were difappointed. Not the leaft fragment of a Gothic window is left: not the mereft mutilation of an arch. It's prefent remains afford as little beauty, as the ruins of a common dwelling. And in all probability the prefent ruin has only been a common dwelling; built from the materials of the ancient abbey. Such at leaft is the tradition of the place. It belonged formerly, we were told, to the family of Haftings; and was loft at play to the earl of Devonfhire: but before the conveyance was prepared; the owner, in the fpirit of revenge, and mortification, fent private orders to have it burnt. — Many a black tale might be unfolded in old houfes, if walls could fpeak.

But the great ftory of this abbey has a virtuous tendency. Within it's walls was once exhibited a fcene more humiliating to human ambition, and more inftructive to human grandeur, that almoft any, which hiftory hath produced. Here the fallen pride of Woolfey retreated from the infults of the world. All his vifions of ambition were now gone; his pomp; and pageantry; and crouded levees. On this fpot he told the liftening monks, the fole attendants of his dying hour, as they ftood around his pallet, that he was come to lay his bones among them: and gave that pathetic teftimony to the truth, and joys of religion, which preaches beyond a thoufand lectures. "If I had ferved God as faithfully as I ferved the king, he would not thus have forfaken my old age."

The death of Woolfey would make a fine moral picture; if the hand of any mafter could give the pallid features of the dying ftatefman that chagrin, that remorfe, thofe pangs of anguifh, which, in thefe laft bitter moments of his life, poffeffed him.—— The point might be taken, when the monks are adminiftring

the

the comforts of religion, which the defpairing prelate cannot feel. The fubject requires a gloomy apartment; which a ray through a Gothic window might juft enlighten; throwing it's force chiefly on the principal figure; and dying away on the reft. The appendages of the piece need only be few, and fimple; little more than the crozier, and red hat, to mark the cardinal, and tell the ftory.

This is not the only piece of Englifh hiftory, which is illuftrated in this ancient town.— Here the houfe is ftill fhewn, where Richard III. paffed the night, before the battle of Bofworth: and there is a ftory of him, ftill preferved in the *corporation-records*, as we were informed by our conductor, (who did not however appear to be a man of deep erudition) which illuftrates the caution and darknefs of that prince's character. — It was his cuftom to carry, among the baggage of his camp, a cumberfome, wooden bed, which he pretended was the only bed he could fleep in. Here he contrived a fecret receptacle for his treafure, which lay concealed under a weight of timber. After the fatal day, on which

Richard fell, the earl of Richmond entered Leicester with his victorious troops. The friends of Richard were pillaged; but the bed was neglected by every plunderer, as useless lumber. — The owner of the house afterwards discovering the hoard, became suddenly rich, without any visible cause. He bought lands; and at length (as our intelligencer informed us) arrived at the dignity of being mayor of Leicester. Many years afterwards, his widow, who had been left in great affluence, was murdered for her wealth by a servant-maid, who had been privy to the affair: and at the trial of this woman, and her accomplices, the whole transaction came to light.

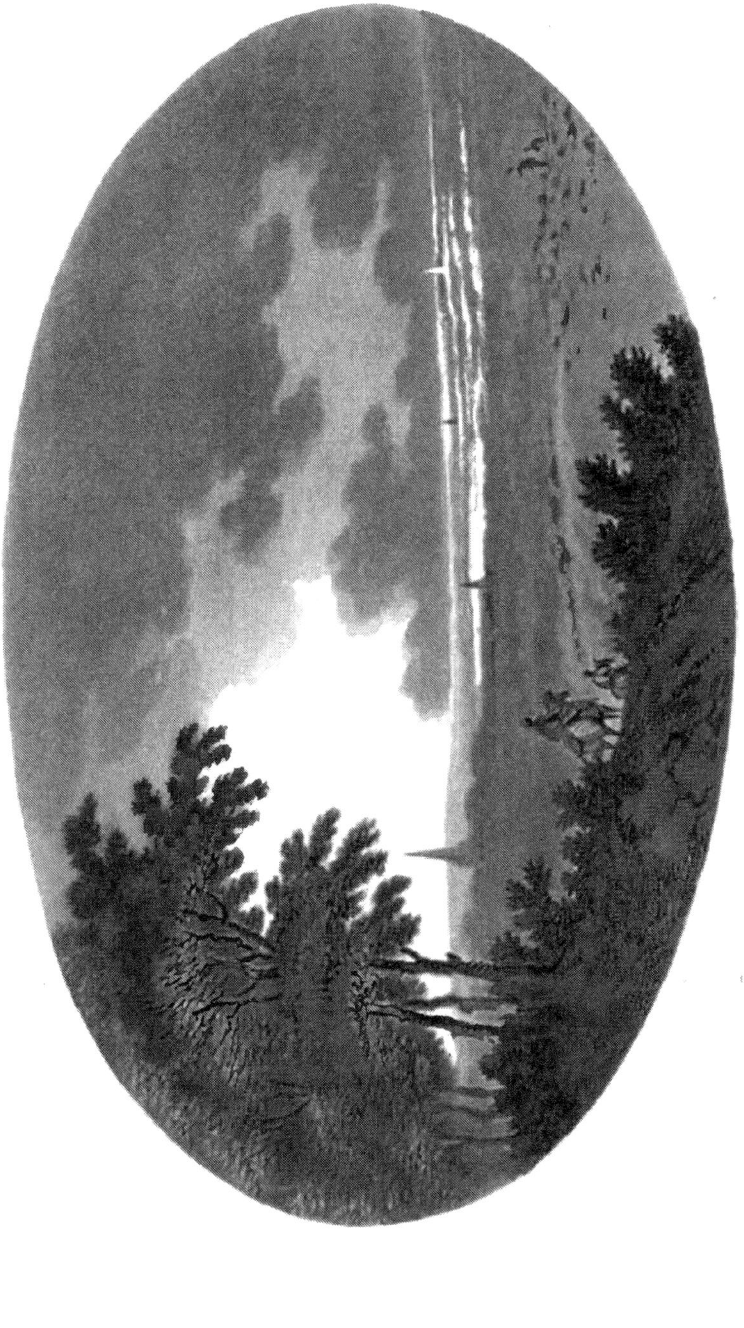

SECT. XXXI.

FROM Leicester the country still continues flat and woody; stretching out into meadows, pastures, and common fields. The horizon, on every side, is generally terminated by spires. Oftener than once we were able to count six, or seven adorning the limits of one circular view.

Of all the countries in England, this is the place for that noble species of diversion, to which the inventive genius of our young sportsmen hath given the name of *steeple-hunting*. In a dearth of game, the chasseurs draw up in a body, and pointing to some conspicuous steeple, set off, in full speed towards it, over hedge and ditch. He who is so happy, as to arrive first, receives equal honour, it is said, as if he had come in foremoſt, at the death of the fox.

In theſe plains, as rich, as they are unpictureſque, we had nothing to obſerve, but the numerous herds of cattle, and flocks of ſheep, which graze them: and in the deficiency of other objects, we amuſed ourſelves with the various forms of theſe animals, and their moſt agreeable combinations.

The horſe in itſelf, is certainly a nobler animal, than the cow. His form is more elegant; and his ſpirit gives fire and grace to his actions. But in a *pictureſque light* the cow has undoubtedly the advantage; and is every way better ſuited to receive the graces of the pencil.

In the firſt place, the lines of the horſe are round and ſmooth; and admit little variety: whereas the bones of the cow are high, and vary the line, here and there, by a ſquareneſs, which is very pictureſque. There is a greater proportion alſo of concavity in them; the lines of the horſe being chiefly convex.

But

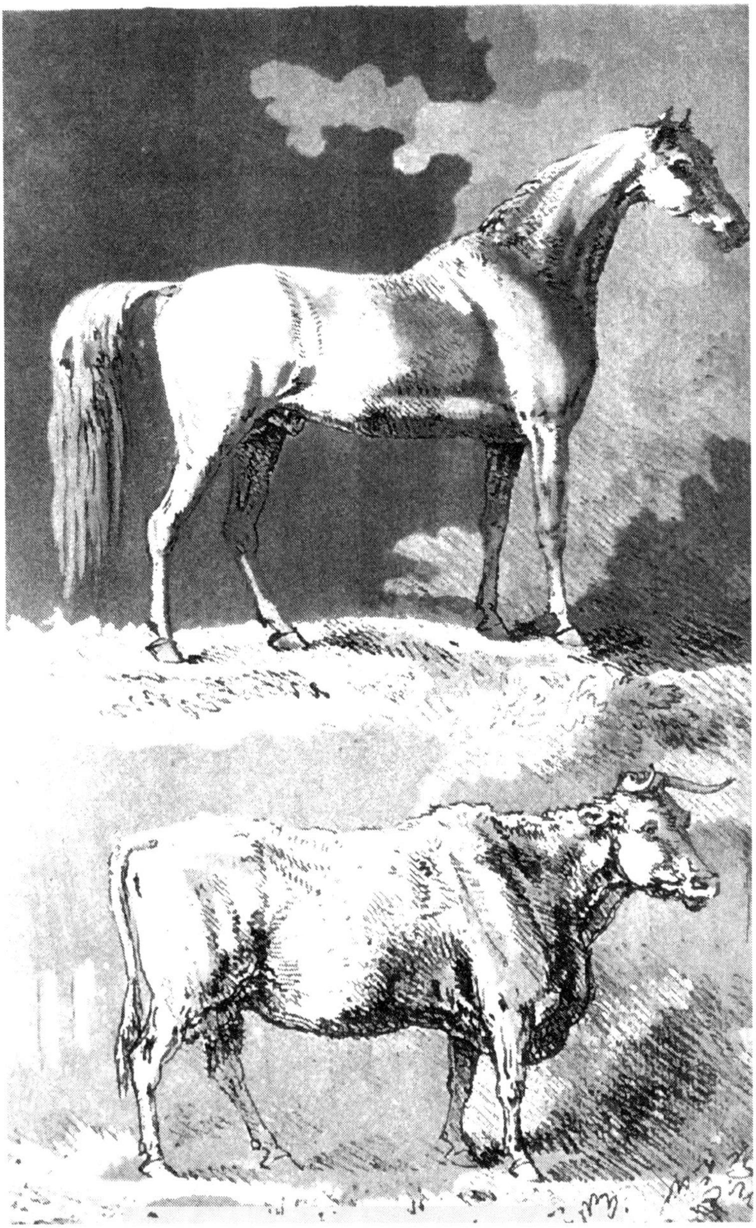

But is not the lean, worn-out horse, whose bones are staring, as picturesque as the cow? In a degree it is; but we do not with pleasure admit the idea of beauty into any deficient form. Prejudice, even in spite of us, rather revolts against such an admission, however picturesque.

The cow also has the advantage, not only in it's picturesque lines; but in the mode of filling them up. If the horse be sleek especially, and have, what the jockies call, a *fine coat*, the smoothness of the surface is not so well adapted to receive the spirited touches of the pencil, as the rougher form and coat of the cow. The very action of licking herself, which is so common among cows, throws the hair, when it is long, into different feathery flakes; and gives it those strong touches, which are indeed the very touches of the pencil. — Cows are commonly the most picturesque in the months of April, and May, when the old hair is coming off. There is a contrast between the rougher, and smoother parts of the coat; and often also a pleasing variety of greyish tints, blended with others of a richer hue. We observe this too in colts, when we see them in a state of nature.

The cow is better adapted also to receive the beauties of light. The horse, like a piece of smooth garden-ground, receives it in a gradual spread: the cow, like the abruptness of a rugged country, receives it in bold catches. And tho in *large objects a gradation of light* is one great source of beauty; yet, in a *small object*, it has not commonly so pleasing an effect, as arises from *smart, catching lights*.

The *colour* of the cow also is often more picturesque. That of the horse is generally uniform. Whereas the tints of the cow frequently play into each other; a dark head melting into lighter sides; and these again being still darker than the hinder parts. Those are always the most beautiful, which are thus tinted with dark colours, harmoniously stealing into lighter. Here and there a few small white spots may add a beauty; but if they run into large blotches, and make a harsh termination between the dark, and light colour, they are disagreeable. The full black also, and full red, have little variety in *themselves*; tho in a *group* all this unpleasant colouring may harmonize.

In the *character*, and *general form* of cows, as well as of horses, there are many degrees of beauty and deformity.

The *character* of the cow is marked chiefly in the head. An open, or contracted forehead; a long or a short visage; the twist of a horn; or the colour of an eyebrow; will totally alter the *character*; and give a sour, or an agreeable air to the countenance. Nor is the head of this animal more characteristic, than it is adapted to receive the graces of the pencil.

With regard to the *general form* of the cow, we are not indeed so exact, as in that of the horse. The points and proportions of the horse are studied, and determined with so much exactness, that a small deviation strikes the eye. In the form of the cow, we are not so learned. If *deformity* be avoided, it is enough. There are two faults particularly in the line of a cow, a *hog-back*, and a *sinking rump*, which are it's most usual blemishes. If it be free from these, and have an harmonious colouring, and a pleasant character, it cannot well be disagreeable.

The

The *bull* and the *cow* differ more in *character* and *form*, than the horse and the mare. They are cast in *different moulds*. The sourness of the head, the thickness and convexity of the neck; the heaviness of the chest, and shoulders; the smoothness of the hip-bones; and the lightness of the hind-quarters, are always found in the bull; and rarely in the cow.

The sheep is as beautiful an animal, as the cow; and as well adapted to receive the graces of painting. Tho it want the variety of colouring: yet there is a softness in it's fleece, a richness, a delicacy of touch, and a sweet tenderness of shadow, which make it a very pleasing object.

The sheep is beautiful in every state, except just when it has past under the sheers. But it soon recovers it's beauty; and in a few weeks loses it's furrowed sides, and appears again in a picturesque dress. It's beauty continues, as the wool increases. What it loses in shape, it gains in the feathered flakiness of it's fleece. Nor is it the least beautiful, when it's sides are a little ragged — when part of it's shape is discovered, and
part

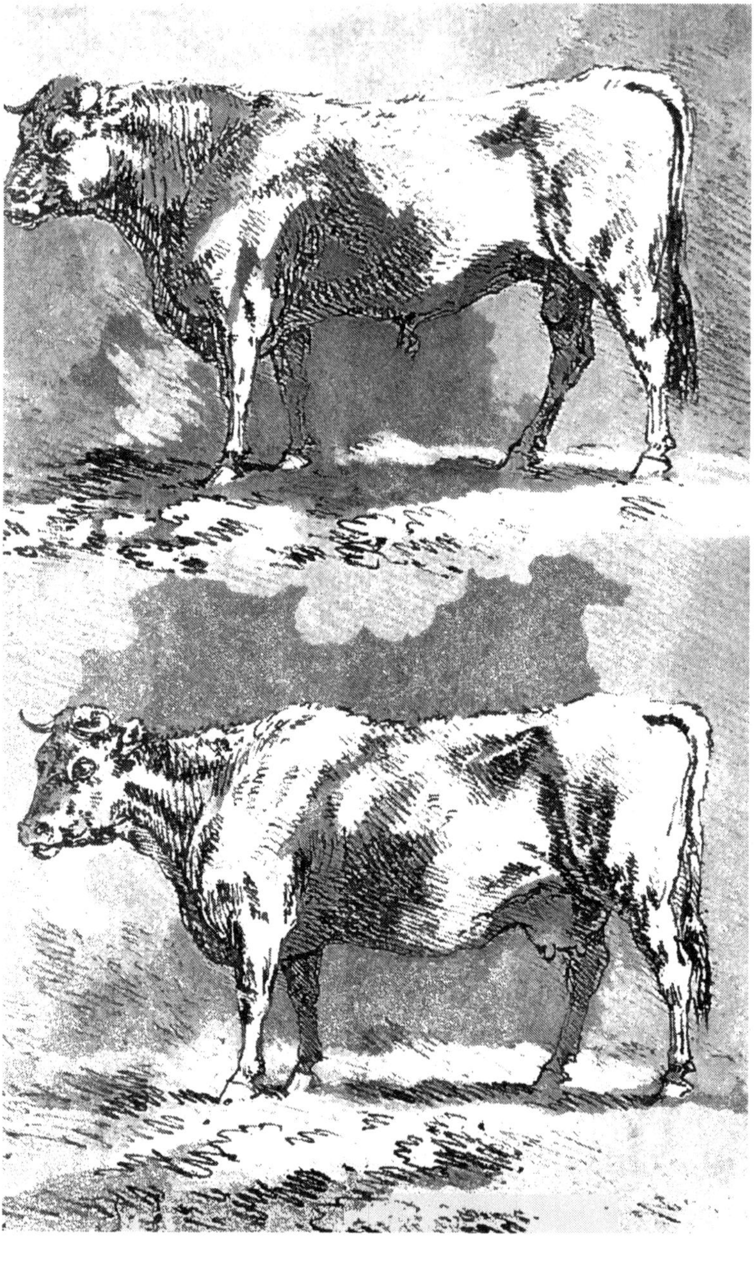

part hid beneath the wool. Berghem delights to repiefent it in this ragged form.

In the *characters*, and *forms* of sheep we obferve little difference. We fometimes fee an unpleafing vifage; and fometimes the difagreeable rounding line, which we have juft called the hog-back: but in an animal fo fmall, the eye is lefs apt to inveftigate *parts*: it rather refts on the *whole appearance*; and the more fo, as sheep being particularly gregarious, are generally confidered as objects in a group.

The obfervations I have made with regard to the beauty of thefe animals, are confirmed by the practice of all the great mafters in animal life, Berghem, Coyp, Potter and others; who always preferred them to horfes and deer, in adorning their rural fcenes.— It is an additional pleafure therefore, that fuch animals, as are the moft ufeful, are likewife the moft ornamental.

Having thus examined the *forms* of thefe picturefque animals, we fpent fome time alfo

in

in examining their moſt agreeble *combinations*.

Cattle are fo large, that when they ornament a foreground, a few are fufficient. Two cows will hardly combine. Three make a good group — either united — or when one is a little removed from the other two. If you increaſe the group beyond three; one, or more, in proportion, muſt neceſſarily be a *little detached*. This detachment prevents heavineſs, and adds variety. It is the ſame principle applied to cattle, which we before applied to mountains, and other objects *.

The ſame rules in grouping may be applied to *diſtant cattle*; only here you may introduce a greater number.

In grouping, contraſted attitudes ſhould be ſtudied. Recumbency ſhould be oppoſed to a ſtanding poſture; forefhortened figures, to lengthened; and one colour, to another. White blotches may enliven a group, tho in a ſingle animal, we obſerved, they are offenſive.

---

* See page 55, vol. ii. &c.

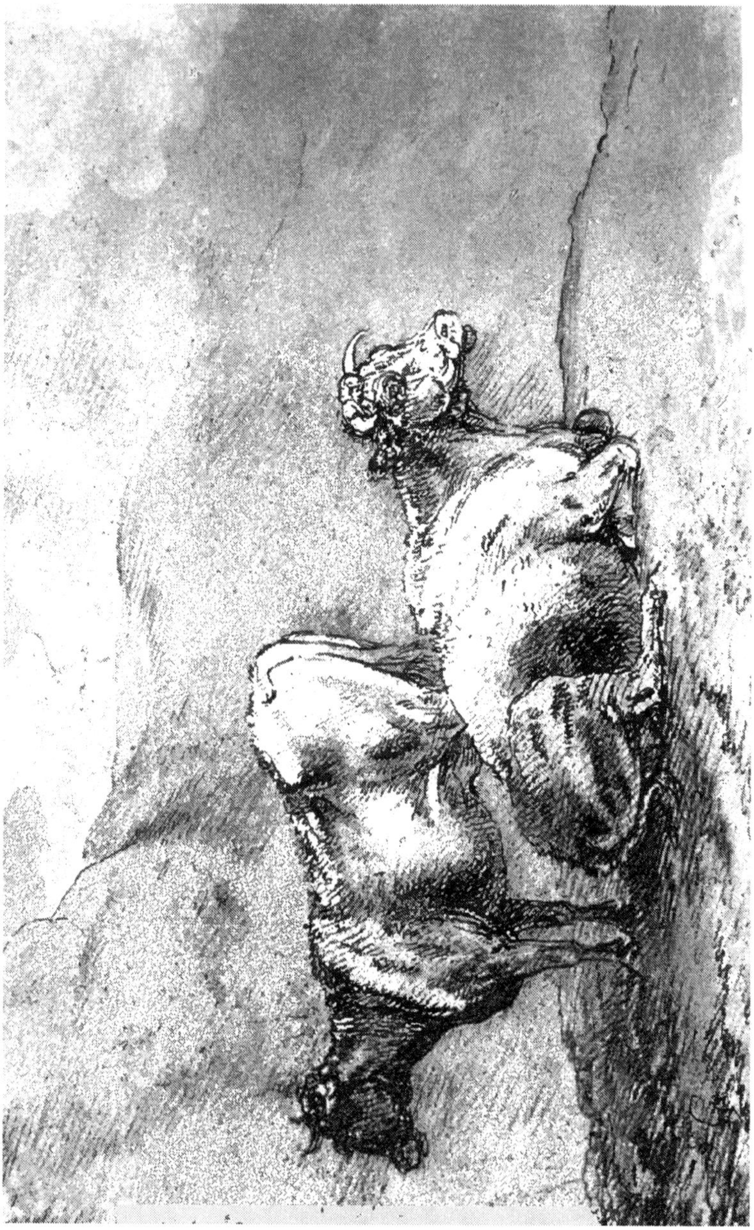

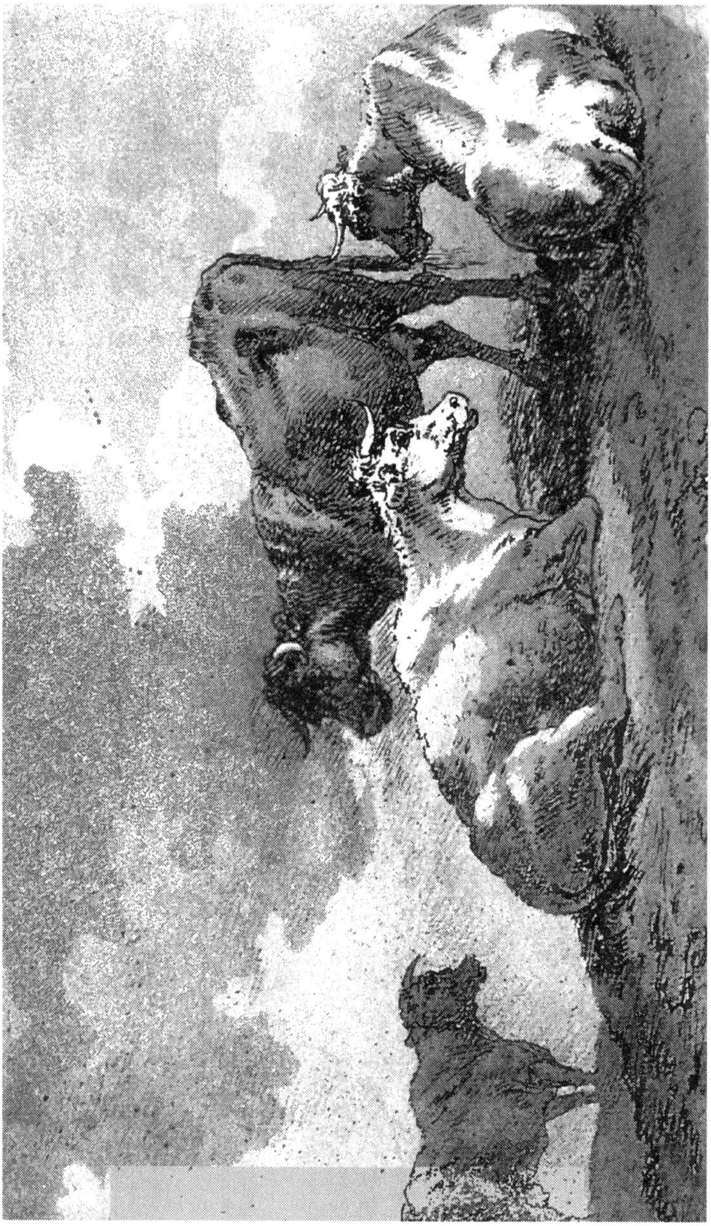

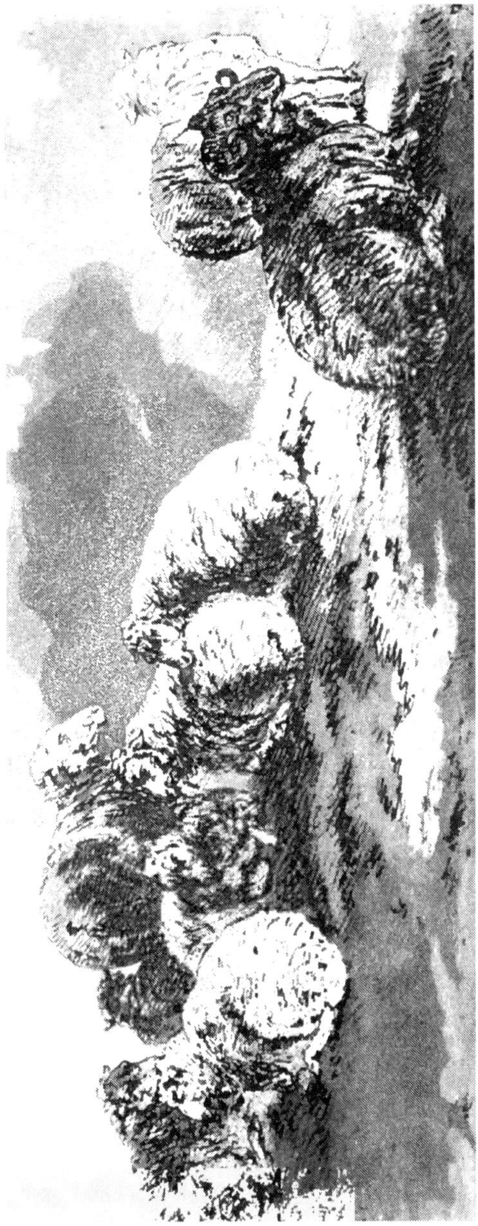

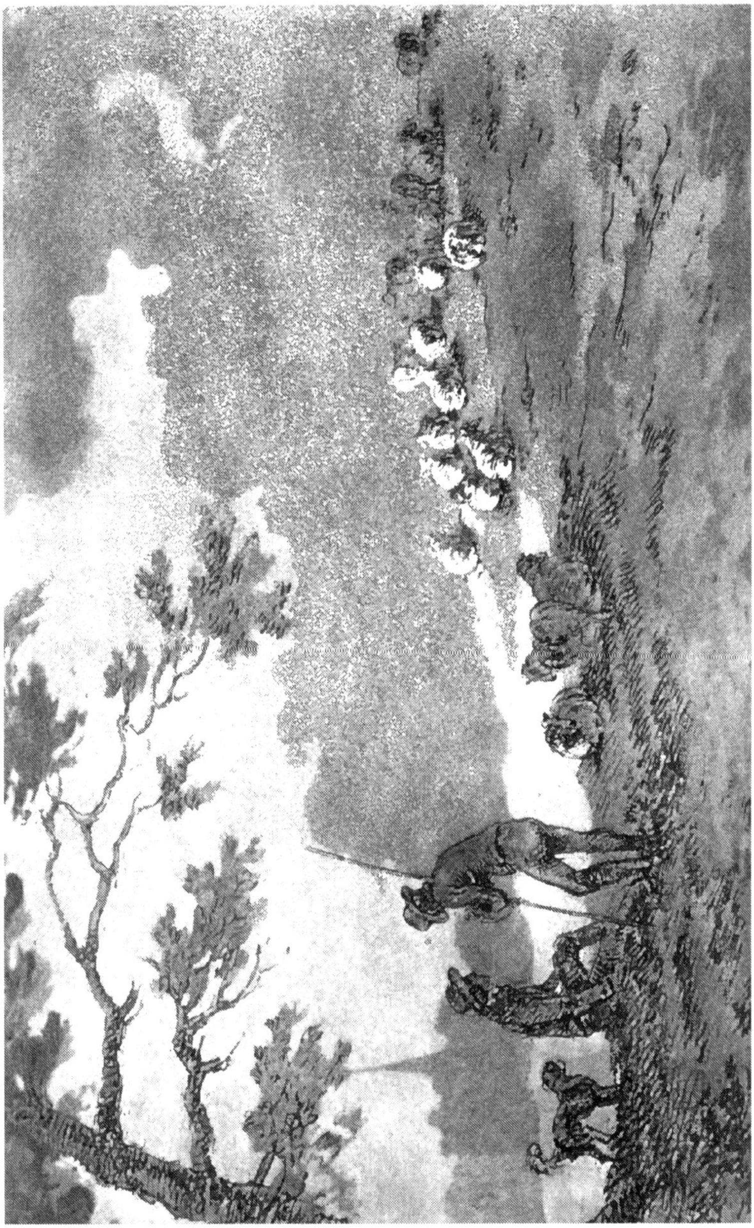

Sheep come under the same rules, only the *foreground*, as well as the *distance*, admits a larger number of these smaller animals. In pastoral subjects sheep are often ornamental, when *dotted about* the sides of *distant* hills. Here little more is necessary, than to guard against regular shapes — lines; circles; and crosses; which large flocks of sheep sometimes form. In combining them however, or, rather scattering them, the painter may keep in view the principle, we have already so often inculcated. They may be huddled together, in one, or more large bodies; from which little groups of different sizes, in proportion to the larger, should be detached.

In favour of the doctrine I have here advanced of the *subordinate group*, I cannot forbear adding the authority of a great master, whose thorough acquaintance with every part of painting hath often, in the course of this work, been observed.

Æneas, landing on the coast of Africa, sees from the higher ground a herd of deer feeding in a valley; and Virgil, who, in the slightest instance, seems ever to have had before his eyes, ideas of picturesque beauty, introduces

introduces the herd, juſt as a painter would have done. From the *larger group* he detaches a *ſubordinate one:*

———————*Tres* litore cervos
Proſpicit errantes, hos *tota armenta* ſequuntur
A tergo,————————

I need not conceal, that ſome commentators have found in theſe three ſtags, which the herd followed, the poet's inclination to ariſtocracy; and that others have ſuppoſed, he meant a complement to the triumvirate. It is the commentator's buſineſs to find out a recondite meaning: common ſenſe is ſatisfied with what is moſt obvious.

It may be obſerved farther, that *cattle* and *ſheep* mix very agreeably *together*; as alſo *young* animals, and *old*. Lambs and calves fill up little interſtices in a group, and aſſiſt the combination.— I may add, that *human figures* alſo combine very agreeably with *animals*. Indeed they generally give a grace to a group, as they draw it to an *apex*.

I need

I need not apologize for this long digreſſion, as it is ſo naturally ſuggeſted by the country, through which we paſſed; and ſo cloſely connected with the ſubject, which we treat. He who ſtudies landſcape, will find himſelf very deficient, if he hath not paid great attention to the choice, and combination, both of animal and human figures.

SECT. XXXII.

LEAVING the plains of Leicesterhire, we entered the county of Northampton, which assumes a new face. The ground begins to rise and fall, and distances to open.

Lord Strafford's gardens, extending a considerable way on the left, are a great ornament to the country.

Lord Hallifax's improvements succeed. They make little appearance from the road: but the road itself is so beautiful, that it requires no aid. It passes through spacious lanes, adorned on each side by a broad, irregular border of grass; and winds through hedge-rows of full-grown oak, which the several turns of the road form into clumps. You have both a good fore-ground, and beautiful views into a fine country, through the boles of the trees. The undreſſed ſimplicity, and native beauty, of ſuch lanes as theſe, exceed the walks of the moſt finiſhed garden.

From Newport-Pagnel the country ſtill continues pleaſant. Before we reach Wooburn, we have a good view of Wooburn-abbey, and of the ſurrounding woods; which decorate the landſcape.

Wooburn-park is an extenſive woody ſcene, and capable of much improvement. We rode through it: but could not ſee the duke of Bedford's houſe; which is ſhewn only on particular days. — But the diſappointment was not great. The *furniture* of all fine houſes is much the ſame; and as for pictures (ſuch is the prevalence of *names*, and faſhion) that ſometimes what are called the beſt collections, ſcarce repay the ceremonies you are obliged to go through in getting a ſight of them.

After

After we leave Wooburn, the views continue ſtill pleaſant; till we meet the chalky hills of Dunſtable. Theſe would disfigure the lovelieſt ſcene. But when we have paſſed theſe glaring heights, the country revives: the riſing grounds are covered with wood, and verdure; and the whole looks pleaſing. About Redburn particularly the country is beautiful; and is thrown into diſtance by large oaks, which over-hang the road.

St. Albans' church, and the ruins about it, make an immenſe pile; of which ſome parts are picturesque. There is a mixture too of brick and ſtone in the building, which often makes a pleaſing contraſt in the tints. Tho there are many remains of beautiful Gothic in this church; there are more deformities of Saxon architecture; particularly the tower, which is heavy, and diſagreeably ornamented. The little ſpire, which ariſes from it, is very abſurd. — Within the church is a monument near the altar, of very curious Gothic workmanſhip.

Among

Among the numerous inhabitants of the fubterraneous regions of this church, lies that celebrated prince, remembered by the name of good duke Humphrey; the youngeft brother of Henry V. He was put to death by a faction, in the fucceeding reign; and was buried fomewhere in this abbey; but his grave was unknown. Having lain concealed near three centuries, he came again to light, not many years ago. By an accident, a large vault was difcovered, in which he was found fole tenant; wrapped in lead, and immerfed in a pickle, which had preferved him in tolerable order.

Near St. Albans ftood the city of Verulam; formerly one of the greateft feats of the Roman empire in Britain. It was facked, and deftroyed by Boadicia, when that heroine, exafperated againft the Romans, cut in pieces their armies. Camden carries the dignity of it into times ftill more remote; and fuppofes it to have been that foreft-town, where Caffibelin defended himfelf againft Cæfar.

Beyond

Beyond Verulam the country grows pleafant. From Barnet, the road enters Finchley-common. The diftance is woody, interfected by an extenfive plain, which is connected with it by a fprinkling of fcattered trees. The parts are large; and the fcenery not unpicturefque.

The firft view of Highgate-hill would make a good diftance, if it were properly fupported by a fore-ground. The view *from* it, is very grand; but is diftracted by a multiplicity of objects.

After this the country is gone. London comes on apace; and all thofe difgufting ideas, with which it's great avenues abound — brick-kilns fteaming with offenfive fmoke — fewers and ditches fweating with filth — heaps of collected foil, and ftinks of every denomination — clouds of duft, rifing and vanifhing, from agitated wheels, purfuing each other in rapid motion — or taking ftationary poffeffion of the road,

road, by becoming the atmofphere of fome cumberfome, flow-moving waggon — villages without rural ideas — trees, and hedge-rows without a tinge of green — and fields and meadows without pafturage; in which lowing bullocks are crouded together, waiting for the fhambles; or cows penned, like hogs, to feed on grains. — It was an agreeable relief to get through this fucceffion of noifome objects, which did violence to all the fenfes by turns: and to leave behind us *the bufy hum of men*; ftealing from it through the quiet lanes of Surry; which leading to no great mart, or general rendezvous, afford calmer retreats on every fide, than can eafily be found in the neighbourhood of fo great a town.

July 3, 1772.

THE END.

Strahan and Prefton,
Printers-Street, London.